AIR VANGUARD 15

JUNKERS Ju 87 STUKA

MIKE GUARDIA

First published in Great Britain in 2014 by Osprey Publishing,
PO Box 883, Oxford, OX1 9PL, UK
PO Box 3985, New York, NY 10185-3985, USA
E-mail: info@ospreypublishing.com

Osprey Publishing is part of the Osprey Group

A CIP catalog record for this book is available from the British Library

Print ISBN: 978 1 4728 0119 7
PDF ebook ISBN: 978 1 4728 0120 3
ePub ebook ISBN: 978 1 4728 0121 0

Index by Mark Swift
Typeset in Sabon
Originated by PDQ Media, Bungay, UK
Printed in China through Asia Pacific Offset Ltd

14 15 16 17 18   10 9 8 7 6 5 4 3 2 1

Osprey Publishing is supporting the Woodland Trust, the UK's leading
woodland conservation charity, by funding the dedication of trees.

www.ospreypublishing.com

IMPERIAL WAR MUSEUM COLLECTIONS

Many of the photos in this book come from the Imperial War Museum's
huge collections which cover all aspects of conflict involving Britain and
the Commonwealth since the start of the twentieth century. These rich
resources are available online to search, browse and buy at
www.iwmcollections.org.uk. In addition to Collections Online, you can
visit the Visitor Rooms where you can explore over 8 million
photographs, thousands of hours of moving images, the largest sound
archive of its kind in the world, thousands of diaries and letters written
by people in wartime, and a huge reference library. To make an
appointment, call (020) 7416 5320, or e-mail mail@iwm.org.uk

Imperial War Museum www.iwm.org.uk

CONTENTS

JUNKERS Ju 87 STUKA

INTRODUCTION

During the early days of *Blitzkrieg*, few aircraft could inspire more terror than the Junkers Ju 87. Nicknamed the "Stuka," (an abbreviation of *Sturzkampfflugzeug* – the German word for "dive-bomber") it quickly became a sign of Nazi air power. With its inverted gull wings and fixed landing gear, the Stuka was one of the most recognizable aircraft of the ETO. Its most potent weapon, however, was psychological. Its dive-activated air siren, known as the "Jericho Trumpet," produced a dreadful wail that could create panic in even the most disciplined of ground units.

Designed by aerospace engineer Hermann Pohlmann, the Stuka had many features that were innovative for the time, including automatic pull-up "dive brakes" which could recover the plane from a dive if its pilot blacked out from the acceleration. Debuting on September 17, 1935, the Stuka's introduction came at a time when Germany was resurging from the turmoil of the Weimar Republic. As Adolf Hitler rebuilt Germany's war machine under the Nazi banner, the Luftwaffe began stacking its arsenal with a fresh inventory of tactical fighters, fighter-bombers, and long-range bombers. The Stuka was accepted into service in 1936, just as the concept of dive-bombing was beginning to take hold in the *Wehrmacht*. By that time, it became apparent that dive-bombers had better accuracy than level bombers and performed better when engaging mobile ground targets.

The Stuka made its combat debut in 1936 with the Luftwaffe's Legion Condor during the Spanish Civil War. Three years later, at the outset of World War II, the Stuka spearheaded the German air campaign over Poland, Norway, and the Low Countries. Around this time, the Ju 87 was also exported to the Bulgarian Air Force, Royal Romanian Air Force, and the Italian *Regia Aeronautica*. The Stuka fought again during the Battle of Britain, but the aerial skirmishes over England revealed several design and performance problems. Its poor maneuverability, low speed, and lack of defensive armaments made it easy prey for Allied fighters. Following the air campaign over Britain, the Stuka required heavy fighter escorts to operate effectively. Despite these setbacks, however, the Stuka went on to achieve success in the Balkans, North Africa, and along the Eastern Front before the Soviets achieved air superiority over the region.

Once the Allied air forces established superiority over the European mainland, the Stuka's effectiveness waned yet again. Nevertheless, Junkers kept the plane in production until 1944 and it remained in service until V-E Day.

During the final years of the conflict, however, the Stuka was largely replaced by ground-attack variants of the Focke-Wulf Fw 190. Throughout its service history, nearly 6,500 Ju 87s were built. Following the end of the war, the Luftwaffe was disbanded and the remaining Stukas, along with the rest of the Nazi-era aircraft, were retired. Today, only a handful of Stukas survive and none are flyable.

DESIGN AND DEVELOPMENT

The story of the Ju 87 begins with the *Luftstreitkräfte* of World War I. Barely a decade after the Wright Brothers' inaugural flight, the concept of using airplanes for military operations had spread throughout Europe. More agile and maneuverable than the hot air balloons of the Franco-Prussian and Napoleonic Wars, the fixed-wing airplane provided a resilient and easily reusable means of performing aerial reconnaissance. However, Kaiser Wilhelm's military planners soon discovered that the airplane could deliver a devastating attack from the third dimension.

Throughout World War I, Germany relied heavily on two classes of bomber aircraft, the fixed-wing *Gotha* series and the military-grade zeppelins. Each, however, met with limited success on the frontlines. The *Gotha* variants were limited in number and their slow maneuverability made them easy prey for Allied fighters. The zeppelins, however, delivered great results during the early bombing campaigns over Britain and Poland. In fact, the zeppelins were initially immune to the enemy's air defenses. Because the pressure of the lifting gas was comparable to the ambient air, the bullet holes had little to no effect.

The Junkers Ju 87 "Stuka" was one of the most recognizable planes of the ETO. During the early days of Blitzkrieg, the Ju 87 spearheaded the aerial campaigns over Poland, Norway, France, and the Low Countries. Although a formidable dive bomber, the Stuka's most potent weapon was psychological: the dive-activated air siren, known as the Jericho Trumpet, produced a dreadful wail that struck fear into the hearts of many Allied troops. (US Navy)

However, once the Allies began using incendiary bullets, the zeppelins' flammable hydrogen gas made them vulnerable targets. To boot, zeppelins were notoriously slow, clumsy, and frequently strayed off course. As they wandered into Allied airspace, they were frequently shot down by French and British fighters. By the end of the war, airships were declared useless as war machines.

Meanwhile, the concept of dive-bombing remained little more than an afterthought. The Royal Air Force had experimented with the concept using their modified SE5a planes and Sopwith Camels but quickly decided that the benefits of dive-bombing did not outweigh the anticipated losses that a unit would incur if it engaged in such tactics.

However, the Germans' perception of dive-bombing was decidedly different. They determined that medium and heavy horizontal bombers could deliver the best results against strategic targets (i.e. enemy cities, infrastructures, and places of industry – targets that could be engaged from higher altitudes). Dive-bombers, on the other hand, would be ideal against tactical targets (i.e. troop formations, supply depots, and field fortifications). Theoretically, a dive-bomber could deliver pinpoint accuracy against these targets, while itself presenting a minimal target to the enemy's air defenses.

The Stuka performs its signature dive during the Battle of Britain. To deliver its bombs on target, the Stuka would turn itself upside down and nose itself into a diving maneuver, sometimes at angles in excess of 80 degrees. It was during the Battle of Britain, however, when the *Luftwaffe* discovered the Stuka's shortcomings. Against an organized aerial resistance, the Stuka's slow airspeed and poor maneuverability made it an easy target for Allied fighters. (Royal Air Force)

Although crippled by the disarmament terms of the Treaty of Versailles, German aircraft companies like Junkers and Heinkel began looking for ways to circumvent the language of the treaty. Junkers, for instance, opened a Swedish subsidiary known as *Flygindustri*. Under the guise of developing civil aircraft in its "straw man" subsidiary, Junkers developed a prototype fighter known as the K 47. A two-seat fighter, the K 47 first flew in 1929 and could carry a 100kg bomb load (typically eight 12.5kg fragmentation bombs). The K 47 underwent extensive trials at the secret German air facility at Lipezk (in the Soviet Union) to test its suitability as a dive-bomber. The K 47 performed remarkably well in these early tests, but its high price tag precluded it from joining the ranks of Germany's small inter-war arsenal.[1]

While Junkers produced and tested the K 47, Heinkel jumped into the fray with the He 50. Heinkel had built the plane at the behest of the Imperial Japanese government. Although Japan had been a longtime ally of the Western powers, she was now restricted by an international treaty that limited the number and tonnage of its capital ships. At the time, US Navy and Marine Corps aviation units were the only ones continuously flying and experimenting with dive-bombers. Japan, surely aware of these developments, and seeking to gain parity with US naval forces, approached Heinkel to develop a dive-bomber. The result was a two-seated, open-cockpit biplane known as the He 50D – exported to Japan in limited numbers. The He 50D became the basis for the Imperial Japanese Navy's Aichi D1A dive-bomber, used extensively against US forces in the Pacific Theater of World War II.

---

1   The few K 47s produced by Junkers were eventually exported to China and the Soviet Union.

In 1932, Heinkel unveiled its second variant of the He 50, which was accepted by the Reichswehr (German defense ministry) as its interim dive-bomber until a better design came along. When the program to develop a new dive-bomber was announced, Hermann Pohlmann, who had been instrumental in designing the K 47 for Junkers, began working on the first of his prototypes for the Ju 87. The timing of Pohlmann's design was fortuitous for him as it coincided with Adolf Hitler's rise to power. When Hitler became Chancellor in 1933, he made the re-militarization of Germany a top priority. With Hermann Göring as the head of Hitler's new air force, the German Air Ministry pushed for the development of a new, two-seated dive-bomber – and Pohlmann's Ju 87 was a top contender.

The first Ju 87 prototype, known simply as the "Ju 87 V1," was powered by a Rolls-Royce Kestrel 12-cylinder engine and sported a twin-tail. Tragically, the V1 crashed during a test flight near Dresden, killing Junkers' veteran test pilot Willy Neuenhofen and his flight engineer Heinrich Kreft. The twin tail fins and rudder could not withstand the gravitational force of the inverted diving maneuvers. Junkers' second prototype, the V2, traded the twin-tail design for a single tailfin. The V2's wings were also fitted with special slats that could be rotated downward at a 90 degree angle, thereby acting as dive brakes. For its battle load, the V2 could accommodate a single 500kg bomb. The singular bomb was fastened to a specially-modified cradle underneath the fuselage. When the pilot hit the bomb release switch during the dive, the cradle hinges would swing forward, providing enough momentum for the bomb to clear the propeller arc before hitting its target. Junkers also replaced the Rolls-Royce engine with a BMW "Hornet" and finally, a Jumo 210 engine. Although the test flight of the second prototype went well, and the pilot praised its performance, Wolfram von Richthofen

An assembly crew at the Junkers Aircraft plant prepares to install the wings on a nearly-completed Ju 87. Junkers had pioneered the concept of all-metal aircraft construction in the 1910s. The company's founder, Hugo Junkers, was imprisoned by the Nazi government in 1934 when the latter seized his company for German re-armament. Junkers died under house arrest the following year. (Bundesarchiv, Bild 101I-642-4711-17A)

A group of Stukas receive their final preparations before leaving the assembly line. Although the Stuka's viability as a dive bomber waned following the Battle of Britain, Junkers continued producing the aircraft until 1944. By the end of the war, however, the Stuka had largely been replaced by ground-attack variants of the Fw 190. (Bundesarchiv, Bild 101I-642-4711-08)

(head of the Luftwaffe's procurement team) told Junkers that the Stuka stood virtually no chance of being selected as the Luftwaffe's primary dive-bomber. Von Richthofen had been wary of the Stuka since the first prototype crashed and thought that even the new-and-improved design was underpowered. The German Air Ministry nearly awarded the dive-bomber contract to Junkers' rival firm Heinkel, as their He 118 seemed to offer a better platform than any of the tested Stukas. However, when the He 118 prototype crashed during its first test flight on July 25, 1936, the Air Ministry announced that the Stuka would become the Luftwaffe's primary dive-bomber.

After the Stuka's selection, Junkers developed a third, fourth, and fifth prototype (V3, V4, and V5 respectively), all of which still had design and performance flaws. The V3 offered the pilot better forward visibility and had a further modified tail unit featuring a full-span elevator. The V4 revealed that the Stuka could take off in 250m, climb to 1,875m in eight minutes with a 250kg bomb load, and reach a cruising speed of 250kph. These performance metrics were below what the Heinkel He 50 had done, and test pilots complained that the navigation and power plant instrumentation were mixed together on the dashboard. This setup, they argued, would make the instruments harder to differentiate during combat. Still, the pilots praised its handling and the resiliency of its airframe. The V4 prototype featured a Jumo 210Aa inverted-Vee engine, and improved the pilot's visibility with a lowered, redesigned cowling and a re-configured canopy. These developments led to the first round of pre-production Ju 87A-0 models which came off the assembly line in the fall of 1936. The Stuka, even with its design drawbacks, had become the Luftwaffe's primary dive-bomber.

Operating the Stuka was a relatively simple affair, but taxiing could be troublesome due to high amount of braking required to steady the aircraft. The airfoil's design also made the plane sensitive to crosswinds. To start the Jumo-series engines, the pilot would open both fuel tanks and give a few strokes to the primer. He would then activate the fuel booster pumps, set the throttle to the "1" notch, and then push down on a handle located to his lower left side for 10 seconds. The pilot would then pull out the handle and repeat the motion until the engine started. As with any plane of the era, the RPMs were regulated while the Stuka was on the ground to prevent it from nosing over.

The Stuka could achieve lift off at approximately 500 yards (457m) at a speed of 116kph. The pilot's procedure for takeoff included switching on the fuel pumps and setting the propeller's pitch lever to "Start." Once airborne, however, the Ju 87 had a relatively slow climbing rate: about 750ft/min (226.8m/min).

To deliver its bombs on target, the Stuka performed a simple vertical diving maneuver. From elevations up to 4,600m, the pilot could locate his

target through a bombsight (known as the *stukavisier*) located on the cockpit floor. Once the pilot had acquired his target, he would move the diving lever to the rear and roll the aircraft over 180 degrees (to where the cockpit was upside down), nosing the Stuka into its dive. Underneath each wing, the Stuka bore a set of automatic dive brakes which could recover the aircraft from its dive in case the pilot "blacked out" from the excessive G-forces brought on by the high acceleration.

The Stuka performed its signature dive at a 60–90 degree angle and at speeds of nearly 500–600kph. The high airspeeds and the steep diving angle greatly increased the Stuka's accuracy, but the pilots often sustained terrible G-forces. During the initial flight tests at Dessau, evaluators learned that a pilot could endure a 4 g pressure with no impairment to vision or other bodily functions. At a force of 5 g, however, pilots began to suffer a "gray out" – meaning that a gray veil would descend over their vision, and images would begin to blur. Further tests revealed that a typical pilot could withstand no more than 8.5 g for three seconds before death or serious injury occurred.

Thus, to mitigate the risk of the G-forces, the Stuka came equipped with an activator light on the contact altimeter to indicate when the pilot should release his bombs (normally at 450m or 1,500ft). After the pilot released his bombs, he would activate the pull-out mechanism by depressing a knob on the center console. Under this procedure, the Stuka automatically pulled up at 6 g. Once the Stuka's nose went above the horizon, the dive brakes automatically retracted, and the throttle was opened. As the pilot regained normal flight, he would reopen the cooling flaps to prevent the Jumo engine from overheating.

Landing the Stuka was easy but nonetheless required full attention from the pilot. The Ju 87 was highly susceptible to nosing over when touching down, thus necessitating a three-point landing. Additionally, the Stuka's undercarriage design was inherently weak. To land the plane, the pilot reduced the Stuka's speed to 150kph during the final approach.

A detailed view of the Stuka's distinctive, inverted gull wings. The inverted wing design was a deliberate attempt by the manufacturer to give the pilot and gunner a better view of the ground situation. Pictured here is one of the few surviving Stukas, currently on display at the Royal Air Force Museum in London, England. (Author's collection)

The Stuka units were structured along the same organizational lines as most German bomber units of the day. The largest mobile and autonomous flight unit was the *Geschwader* (similar to the bomber wings of the United States Army Air Forces). Every *Geschwader* was given an operational prefix based on its purpose. The dive-bomber units were therefore called *Sturzkampfgeschwader*, abbreviated as *Stuka Geschwader* or more commonly, StG.

The Geschwader's first subordinate unit was the *Gruppe*. Typically, there were three *Stukagruppen* in each *Geschwader*. All the *Gruppen* organized within a *Geschwader* were designated by Roman numerals: I, II, III etc. For example, the 2nd *Gruppe* of the 77th *Sturzkampfgeschwader* would be designated II./StG 77. Each *Gruppe* contained three *Staffel* units (plural: *Staffeln*). The *Staffel* was the equivalent of a squadron and normally carried 12 to 16 aircraft. The *Staffel* itself was further divided into three *Schwärme* (singular: *Schwarm*). In bomber units, a *Schwarm* was subdivided into a *Kette* of three aircraft.

But, as it turned out, creating an organizational scheme for the Stuka units was the simple part. Throughout World War II, the greater challenge for the Luftwaffe was finding and training suitable pilots and ground crews for the Ju 87 – especially as it evolved from a dive-bomber into a ground-attack aircraft. Generalmajor Hubertus Hitschhold, a prominent Stuka ace and recipient of the Knight's Cross of the Iron Cross, recalled the training and evaluation for pilots entering the Ju 87 program:

> The supply of pilots for day ground attack operations was good. Those pilots not entirely suitable were detected in time in the schools. It proved to be very profitable for COs of primary schools who had themselves been ground attack pilots to have influence on the selection of men for ground attack forces. The shoving off of poor pilots [i.e. failed fighter pilots] with the designation of 'suitable for ground attack work' was thereby avoided.
>
> But the supply of new pilots alone could not cover the needs of the operational units. Therefore, the pilots from other branches had to be grabbed. Fighter pilots who had been relieved because of lack of suitability and achievement failed just as badly in the ground attack arm. Only those fighter pilots who were relieved because of altitude trouble, and who were otherwise good, became good ground attack pilots. Reconnaissance units continually made available surplus officer pilots. These pilots in general proved good in ground attack operations, since they brought with them as a result of their reconnaissance experience a tactical understanding of ground attack missions.
>
> Former bomber pilots did not usually prove good ground attack pilots. They lacked the practical eye for recognizing targets in the air and on the ground, and the necessary maneuverability for flying formations.
>
> The night ground attack units were supplied with relieved pilots so far as they had no character deficiencies, some from transport units, and some from liaison units. Since enough of these pilots were available, the need could be covered after careful selection.

Every Stuka unit employed a variety of pilot leaders and technical crew. At the lowest operational level, the *Schwarm* leaders were selected based on experience in formation flying and had to possess a working knowledge of target identification. At the next operational tier, pilot officers became *Staffel* commanders only when they had enough combat experience or had otherwise proven themselves capable. Under this revised merit system, younger officers were frequently selected as *Staffel* commanders, while older officers in the same *Gruppe* remained ordinary pilots or *Schwarm* leaders. At the highest

levels of command, the *Gruppe* and *Geschwader* commanders were often selected from the older and proven *Staffel* leaders. In the ground attack units, the *Staffel* and *Gruppe* commanders who were in line for promotions were first sent to serve, respectively, as *Gruppe* and *Geschwader* commanders of training units. This allowed the pilots to get acquainted with their new responsibilities at the higher echelon. Hence, when these pilots returned to take command of an operational unit, they brought with them the administrative knowledge needed for the new job. However, this training scheme was not always possible simply because of the Luftwaffe's manpower needs and the high attrition rate among Stuka pilots as the war dragged on.

The Ju 87 Technical Officers (TOs) were, initially, pilots who had taken the requisite maintenance courses to become Stuka mechanics. In the early days of the war, it was considered essential that every pilot and commander have a working knowledge of the Stuka's technical matters. In most cases, however, the TOs did not enjoy being grounded and flew along during missions rather than focus exclusively on their technical duties. To correct this skill gap, however, the Luftwaffe began employing older mechanics and medically grounded pilots (retrained as technicians) which proved to be an effective measure. Hubertus Hitschhold also recalled that the "strength of maintenance personnel was usually the same as in the Fighter units. The only differences were that there were more bomb personnel and fewer ordinary ordnance personnel."

Staff officers within the Stuka units included adjutants, operations and intelligence officers, and meteorologists. Ideally, the Luftwaffe wanted its Ju 87 pilots to serve as adjutants because it prepared them for the administrative duties of a *Gruppe* commander. More often, however, grounded pilots filled these roles as the flying officers had to stay in the sky to beat back the Allied air forces. Other grounded pilots, along with some reservists, became the operations and intelligence officers. "Former reconnaissance pilots were found best suited for intelligence work," said Hitschhold. "For ground attack units,

A German ground crew works on the Stuka's massive Jumo engine. The Jumo engine was designed and built by Junkers Aircraft. Its two main variants were the Jumo 210 and 211, both of which were 12-cylinder engines. Featured aboard many Luftwaffe aircraft (including variants of the Heinkel He 111 and the Messerschmitt Me 264), the Jumo 211 series was the most-produced German aero engine of World War II. (Bundesarchiv, Bild 101I-378-0037-16)

intelligence officers were first introduced toward the end of 1944. In the west, intelligence officers were necessary for *Geschwader* and *Gruppe* Staffs. On the Eastern Front, one intelligence officer sufficed for one *Geschwader*. It proved to have been a mistake to have omitted intelligence work in the units." Lastly, meteorologists were used only in night attack units. They were considered superfluous in the day bombardment units because weather forecasts were generally provided by higher headquarters and missions rarely went beyond 150km from the air base.

In flight, the Ju 87's priority targets were as follows:

- Ground troops
- Heavy weapon emplacements
- Enemy vehicles
- Field fortifications
- Headquarters and troop billets
- Bridges
- Airfields
- Railroad targets including locomotives
- Shipping targets

A Ju 87 prepares for another bombing raid against Soviet positions, March 1942. Along the Eastern Front, the Germans made stunning advances into Soviet territory and gathered a string of impressive victories during Operation *Barbarossa*, the battle of the Kerch Peninsula, and battle of Sevastopol. During that first year of the Eastern campaign, the Stuka flew thousands of sorties against Soviet ground forces. (Bundesarchiv, Bild 101I-393-1409-02)

The Stuka could effectively engage enemy troops with small fragmentation bombs ranging from 1 to 10kg. For heavy weapons (including field guns, artillery, and anti-aircraft guns) the Luftwaffe recommended 50, 70, and 250kg fragmentation bombs. Utility vehicles and lightly-armored vehicles could easily be destroyed with bombs of 1–70kg. Tanks, however presented a different challenge. Hubertus Hitschold recalled that "Bombing with 50–500kg bombs was not successful because the tanks presented too small a target. Destruction with such bombs was only accomplished if the bomb hit within 15ft of the tank." The smaller 4kg hollow-charge bombs, however, were highly effective against tanks as were the autocannons equipped with armor-piercing rounds. Field fortifications and troop quarters were prime candidates for the 250kg bomb.

Bridges, however, proved to be among the most difficult targets – "and usually brought little success," Hitschold added. Stone and concrete bridges could only be damaged by direct hits from the heavier-grade bombs and then only temporarily. Hitschold also said that steel bridges were particularly troublesome because their framework "often dissipated the blast effect." Except in cases of fortuitous first hits, "steel bridges normally took multiple bombing runs to destroy."

A **DIVE SEQUENCE**

The Stuka's signature dive pattern. After acquiring the target through a floor-mounted bombsight, the pilot rolled the Stuka through 180 degrees and began the dive, usually reaching 500–600kph. An altimeter-activated indicator told the pilot when to release his bombs. The automatic dive brakes would pull the plane out of its dive if the pilot blacked out from the high G-forces.

INSET:

The dive-activated air siren, known as the "Jericho Trumpet," produced a terrifying wail that could cause fear and panic in even the most resilient ground forces.

When the Stuka went into action against enemy airfields, the main point of attack was the destruction of formed aircraft with 1 to 10kg bombs. Railroad bombing was another high priority for the Stuka. Hitschold again: "Main points of attack were tracks in and out of stations, and easily blocked sections like bridges and cuts. Attacks on open stretches of track and on unoccupied stations brought no lasting effect. Most practical for these purposes were bombs of 250kg or more. Trains in motion were wrecked with heavy bombs and the troops streaming out of them were strafed and bombed with small fragmentation bombs."

In combat, the Stuka generally flew three types of missions: a concentrated attack, rolling attack, or a free sweep attack. In a concentrated attack, Stuka units were combined and took flight to engage a clearly defined set of targets. These attacks were flown in direct support of the ground forces and came to be known as "flying artillery" – softening up the enemy's targets ahead of the friendly force's main advance. "The mission," as Hitschhold recalled, "was to destroy the enemy or to injure his morale so that after that the ground troops would have little or no defense to contend with. This was only possible when the Army, immediately after the concentrated attack from the air, took advantage of its effect by launching an attack of its own. Similarly, such concentrated attacks make easier the disengaging movements of friendly troops." In other instances, these concentrated attacks could also be carried out in indirect support of ground forces (e.g. against heavily occupied airfields, rail stations, and infrastructure targets).

Rolling attacks were continuous operations. After the German ground forces had seized a particular area, the Ju 87s would patrol the sky (in *Staffel* size or larger), looking for targets of opportunity beyond the forward edge of the battle area. The intent, according to Hitschold, was to "paralyze every movement of enemy troops against friendly troops and to destroy every enemy concentration of forces." To effect these rolling attacks, the Stukas often stood ready with an assortment of bombs pre-loaded, enough to accommodate whatever mission was next. The ultimate goal was to destroy the enemy's follow-on echelons before he had the chance to defend himself against an aerial attack or maneuver against the assaulting ground forces.

The free sweep attacks were carried out simultaneously with ground combat operations. Their objectives were, as Hitschhold said, "broad and bold, like continuous support of a tank spearhead or flank cover for a breakthrough wedge." The free sweep attacks were normally carried out at the *Kette* or *Staffel* level and operated as a hunter-killer team. By this, the Stukas would hunt individual targets (i.e. tanks, light-armored vehicles, troop emplacements) which could simultaneously suppress the enemy while keeping continuous observation over him. By closely coordinating with the ground forces or the forward headquarters, the Ju 87s' free sweep attack guaranteed disruption of the enemy's battle rhythm. Of course, whether conducting a consolidated, rolling, or free sweep attack, the Stuka could only be effective if the enemy forces had not gained air superiority.

A Stuka flies over Stalingrad with the Volga River in the background. During the campaign, Ju 87s from StG 1, StG 2, and StG 77 flew more than 1,000 sorties against the entrenched Soviets on the west bank of the Volga. The three *Stukageschwader* flew an average of 500 sorties per day, losing an average of one Stuka every day of the campaign. (Bundesarchiv, Bild 183-J20509)

TECHNICAL SPECIFICATIONS AND PRODUCTION VARIANTS

Throughout its service life, the Ju 87 retained the same basic design and construction. With every successive variant, minor modifications and upgrades were made, but the airframe itself remained virtually unchanged.

To effect their design for a resilient dive-bomber, Junkers Aircraft used a construction technique that their founder, Hugo Junkers, had pioneered two decades earlier. The cantilever design, as it were, consisted of a single beam anchored at only one end. This design facilitated carrying a structure's load without any external braces or modifications. Hugo Junkers adapted this technique to strengthen his monoplane designs in the mid-1910s. To that point, most airplanes had been constructed as biplanes (i.e. two wings supported by a network of wires and struts). However, this configuration created considerable drag and negatively affected the planes maneuverability in combat.

Thus, to eliminate drag and improve his planes' aerodynamics, Junkers sought to eliminate all the external bracing structures and have the weight of the wings carried within. The resulting adaptation was called a "cantilever" which consisted of a single beam, known as the main spar, which ran the length of the wingspan, usually near the leading edge of the wing. During flight, the main spar carried the upward bending loads (created by lift) and the drag loads through the fuselage to the other wing. Ultimately, this design eliminated the need for any external load-bearing structures, and greatly improved the aerodynamic qualities of the Junkers airframes.

Along with the cantilever design, Junkers Aircraft developed a unique metallurgical configuration for its dive-bomber. The airframe was constructed of *duralumin*, an aluminum alloy consisting of copper, magnesium, and manganese. Just as he had done with the cantilever design, Hugo Junkers had also pioneered duralumin for aviation use – creating a prototype aircraft with a duralumin corrugated skin in 1916. While the Ju 87 featured a duralumin body, certain parts of the plane required stronger materials to withstand the normal wear of everyday flight. Subsequently, these parts of the airframe were constructed with stronger magnesium alloys. To facilitate easier maintenance, Junkers avoided welding parts of the Stuka wherever possible, opting instead for cast and molded parts.

The fuselage itself was built in two oval-shaped sections joined along the main chord. Though not a true monocoque design, the Ju 87's cantilever construction allowed for a simpler structure of internal formers and stringers. Formers (or frames) run perpendicular to the horizontal axis of the plane and typically give the aircraft its shape. Stringers (also referred to as longerons) are long strips of material, running the longitudinal direction of the aircraft, fastened to the plane's skin. Aboard the Stuka, the formers were constructed in a Z-pattern to facilitate easier inspection of stringers. The stringers themselves were U-shaped and were fastened to the duralumin skin by two congruent lines of rivets, uniform throughout the plane. At each frame junction, a curved bracket was riveted to each former and stringer. The stringers were riveted closer together in the lower sections of the fuselage while the strongest formers were placed near the spars. This modified configuration of formers and stringers was designed to reinforce the areas of the plane that would endure the most stress during air combat maneuvering. The overall design of the fuselage also

British troops inspect a Ju 87B that was forced to make an emergency landing in the North African desert, December 1941. Throughout the North African campaign, the British Army captured a handful of Stukas that were forced to land behind enemy lines. (Imperial War Museum, E 3900E)

ensured that Stuka could withstand the excessive G-forces during its dive and subsequent recovery, both of which occurred at high speeds.

The cockpit was a simple design accommodating the pilot and rear gunner seated back-to-back under the cover of a transparent canopy. In the event of a bailout, the entire canopy could be easily jettisoned by either crewman. The two crewmen were separated by a large anti-crash ring constructed of cast magnesium. This prevented the cockpit from being crushed if the plane rolled over during take-off or landing. In the earliest versions of the Stuka, the pilot was responsible for both flying the aircraft and operating the radio. Beginning with the Ju 87B, however, radio responsibilities shifted to the gunner, thereby freeing the pilot to concentrate on his flying and tactical engagements. Both crewmen were protected from the V-12 engine by a firewall made of asbestos, situated in front of the wings near the fuel tanks.

The Ju 87's wings were a double-wing (*doppelflüger*) construction. This was a standard feature on Junkers' aircraft at the time. The *doppelflüger* design used full-span ailerons that were hinged just below the trailing edge of the wing. The wings also featured hydraulic-operated flaps which were divided into three sections along the length of the wing – a design that first appeared aboard Junkers's own Ju 52 transport a few years earlier. The Ju 87's wings were indeed the most distinctive part of the plane. Their inverted "gull wing" shape was a deliberate attempt by the designer to create better ground visibility for the pilot and permit a shorter undercarriage height. These gull wings were constructed in three sections – center, port, and starboard. The center section was a critical part of the fuselage as it housed the undercarriage equipment, not the least of which was the fixed landing gear. The port and starboard sections of the wing were attached to the center section by ball-and-socket joins along the spar. To achieve the inverted gull wing shape, the center section

B **Ju 87B**

The standard Ju 87B with the Iron Cross roundel. The Ju 87B was the first mass-produced variant of the Stuka and the first to be exported to other Axis nations. Much of the Ju 87's body was constructed with duralumin, a heavy-grade alloy consisting of copper, magnesium, and manganese. To facilitate maintenance and overhaul, most of the Stuka's airframe segments were interchangeable.

of the wing was depressed to an anhedral angle of 12 degrees and a dihedral angle of 8 degrees. To accommodate the unorthodox wing design, Junkers built the Ju 87's wings around two spars. Each spar had L-section rims that were riveted together via flat plate covers. The duralumin skinning was then flush-riveted to the wing frame. The wings were also mounted low to facilitate higher airspeeds at lower altitudes.

With the exception of the prototypical Ju 87 V1, all successive Stukas had a single-finned vertical stabilizer. These tailfins were little more than a simple cantilever fin and rudder. The fin and rudder were square-cut while the tailplane wings were rectangular. The tailfin trimmings were mechanically linked to the flaps. Meanwhile the elevators and rudder could be adjusted during flight via trim tabs. The automatic pull-out device, another distinctive feature of the Ju 87, was actually a function of its tail unit design. A control surface on the starboard elevator would automatically come under tension once the dive brakes were activated. However, once the pilot engaged the bomb release, it released the tension on the starboard elevator and plane would begin to recover from its dive.

The Jumo engine, in its various incarnations aboard the Stuka, was mounted atop two support frames held up by internal struts and placed between two magnesium castings. The Jumo was secured to the engine well by four ball-and-socket joints. Maintenance on the Jumo-series engine was a simple affair. According to most mechanics, the Jumo could be removed from the airframe within 20 minutes. The engine itself was water-cooled (supplied by a 10-liter water tank) and operated on a fuel injector that delivered fuel from two 240-liter tanks. The Stuka also came equipped with an auxiliary manual pump to use if the fuel injector failed. The powertrain was attached to a three-blade Jumo-Hamilton HPA III propeller that featured an automatic regulator for RPMs.

The main armament on the Ju 87 was its onboard machine guns. The pilot operated twin MG 17 machine guns, one located underneath each wing. Firing 7.92mm ammunition from a 500-round feed belt, the MG 17 was a mainstay of the Luftwaffe during World War II. Aside from Stuka, the MG 17 also flew aboard the Messerschmitt Bf 109, Focke-Wulf Fw 190, and Heinkel He 111. The rear gunner fired an MG 15, which also a 7.92mm gun, but with a lower rate of fire and lower muzzle velocity.

Ju 87A

Specifications	
Crew	2
Length	10.8m
Height	3.9m
Wingspan	13.8m
Wing Area	31.9sq m
Tare Weight	2,300kg
Load Weight	3,400kg
Engine	Jumo 210-series, 12 cylinder
Maximum Speed	320km/h
Range	1,000km
Service Ceiling	8,100m

The Ju 87A (nicknamed "Anton," in accordance with the German phonetic alphabet) differed only slightly from its pre-production prototypes. It retained the single tail fin and, at first, also retained the Jumo 210 engine. The first Anton variant, the A-0, had an all-metal airframe. Its fuselage was lowered along with the gunner's station to allow the gunner a better field of vision. The A-series also featured two radio antennas which were arranged in a V-shaped configuration away from the cockpit. However, in successive variants of the Stuka, the double radio antennae were replaced by a single antenna which stood vertical just outside the rear gunner's station. A-series planes also featured the FuG VII radio, a system which was also carried aboard the Focke-Wulf Fw 190. The FuG VII enabled the crew to transmit and receive radio traffic over long distances.

In the spring of 1937, the A-0 variants underwent extensive testing with various bomb loads but Wolfram von Richthofen, the Stuka's perennial skeptic, pointed out that the Jumo 210 rendered the aircraft horribly underpowered. This led to the installation of an improved Jumo 210D power plant, and thus a newer variant, the A-1. The A-1 also carried an offensive load of one 458kg bomb if the pilot flew solo, or one 250kg bomb if the plane flew with its standard two-man crew. A further variant, the A-2, upgraded the radio system with an Ei V intercom for voice transmission between the pilot and rear gunner.

Ju 87B

Specifications	
Crew	2
Length	11m
Height	3.9m
Wingspan	13.8m
Wing Area	31.9sq m
Tare Weight	2,750kg
Load Weight	4,250kg
Engine	Jumo 211-series, 12 cylinder
Maximum Speed	380km/h
Range	500–600km
Service Ceiling	8,000m

A German crewman paints a winter camouflage pattern on the wings of a Ju 87 for service along the Eastern Front. Every Stuka nonetheless had to retain the Luftwaffe roundels of the Iron Cross and the swastika. (Bundesarchiv, Bild 101I-665-6815-10)

The Ju 87B (nicknamed "Berta") was the first mass-produced variant. The first of the B-series, the Ju 87B-1, featured a larger Jumo 211D engine producing 1,184hp, along with an updated fuselage. The 211D engine permitted the Stuka to carry bomb loads of up to 1,000kg. After successfully testing the B-1 in the skies over Spain, the Nazis increased production to 60 units per month. Thus, by the onset of World War II, the Luftwaffe had more than 300 B-1s in service.

The B variants were also the first to feature the "Jericho Trumpet," the notorious air siren which produced the Ju 87's distinctive wail. During the early days of Blitzkreig, the dreadful siren struck fear and panic into even the most resilient ground forces. As the war dragged on, however, the air siren lost its shock value. Thus by 1943, the Jericho Trumpet had been removed from most of the remaining Stukas. The origin of the Jericho Trumpet remains the subject of debate. Some historians claim that the Stuka pioneer Ernst Udet thought of the idea, while others claim it was Adolf Hitler's invention. Regardless, the Stuka's Jericho Trumpet was a powerful tool of psychological warfare and, in many ways, came to symbolize the aerial campaigns of Blitzkrieg.

For the B-1, Junkers redesigned the engine cowling with a new air intake and radiator. The wheel fairings from the A-series planes were replaced with simpler versions. The spats could be removed if the Ju 87 were operating in rough terrain. Towards the end of the war, some Stuka units opted to remove the wheel coverings altogether. The B-1's undercarriage was also reinforced to reduce the chance of the landing gear being sheared off while landing on rough surfaces. Following the Ju 87B-1, the B-2 variant included a ski-equipped version and a new oil hydraulic system to close the cowl flaps. The B-2 was also the first variant to see a viable export market. Italy, Hungary, Bulgaria, and Romania each received sizeable quantities of the Stuka B-2. Production of the B variants ended in October 1940.

Ju 87C

Specifications	
Crew	2
Length	11m
Height	3.9m
Wingspan	13.8m
Wing Area	31.9sq m
Tare Weight	2,760kg
Load Weight	5,840kg
Engine	Jumo 211-series, 12 cylinder
Maximum Speed	332km/h
Range	580km
Service Ceiling	7,000m

In early 1938, Junkers developed a prototype for the Ju 87C. The C variant was intended to be a naval torpedo-bomber and dive-bomber for the *Kriegsmarine*. The first prototypes were built on the Ju 87B airframes and were powered by a comparable Jumo-series engine. The first prototype, the V10, featured the same fixed-wing design as the earlier Ju 87A and B versions. However, the second C-series prototype featured folding wings to accommodate its stowage aboard Germany's planned aircraft carriers. During its initial

C

1: Ju 87A-2
The Ju 87A was the first production variant of the Stuka. Even with its design flaws, however, the Stuka was the best all-round dive bomber that the German aircraft industry had to offer. The Ju 87A had a very short operational history before being replaced by the Ju 87B.

2: Ju 87B-1
The Ju 87B was the first mass produced variant of the Stuka. This aircraft carries the insignia of StG 51. It saw action during the invasion of France in 1940.

3: Ju 87D-1
This Stuka, belonging to Walter Seigel (the commander of StG 3), shows a variant of the desert camouflage.

4: Ju 87R-2
This Stuka, from StG 2, shows a typical desert camouflage pattern with a decorative serpent for added psychological effect.

1

2

3

4

testing phase from 1938–39, the Ju 87C made nearly 1,000 arrest wire landings on dry land. Although the test flights and practice landings were successful by Luftwaffe standards, all orders for the C variants were nonetheless cancelled as the Blitzkrieg invasion began. By mid-1940, production of the Ju 87C was converted to the newer Ju 87R variant (see below).

Ju 87D

Specifications	
Crew	2
Length	11.5m
Height	3.9m
Wingspan	15m
Wing Area	33.6sq m
Tare Weight	3,940kg
Load Weight	6,600kg
Engine	Jumo 211-series, 12 cylinder
Maximum Speed	400km/h
Range	1,000km
Service Ceiling	7,320m

A Stuka is fitted with skis for landing gear, December 22, 1941. The German forces were grossly under-prepared for the harsh Russian winters. With heavy snow and ice covering the temporary airfields, skis were often the only means for a Stuka to land safely. (Bundesarchiv, Bild 101I-392-1334-04)

Following the Battle of Britain in 1940, it was clear to the Luftwaffe that their prized dive-bomber was no match for the Allied fighters. Nevertheless, Nazi Germany had little choice but to continue producing and upgrading the Stuka; it was the only dive-bomber available and there were no better designs on the drawing board as of yet.

Seeking to improve their dive-bomber's capability, Junkers developed the D-series Ju 87. The D variant featured an aerodynamically refined cockpit

with increased visibility for the pilot and rear gunner. The D-series' nose was re-contoured by moving the oil cooler below the engine while the oil coolant radiator was re-positioned below the wings. Junkers also increased the engine output to over 1,400hp and nearly quadrupled the bomb capacity from the previous B-series model (500kg to more than 1,800kg). Fuel capacity also increased to 800 liters with an additional 300 liters provided by an optional pair of drop tanks. The additional fuel capacity gave the D-series model a flight time of nearly two and a half hours while the external drop tanks brought the D-series flight time to a total of four hours. Further modifications to the D variant included the installation of a new VS 11 propeller with paddle blade configuration, an improved armor configuration, a prototype torpedo-bomber version, the adoption of two 20mm M6 151/20 cannons, and an increase in the rear gunner's ammunition supply from 1,000 rounds to 2,000. As in the C-series, the D variants featured an undercarriage removal system that permitted the landing gear to be replaced with skis or pontoons.

Shortly after Junkers unveiled the D-1 model, the company introduced the upgraded D-2. It was essentially identical to the D-1, but featured a stronger tailfin wheel and additional equipment for glider towage. A further variant, the D-3 removed the Jericho Trumpet from the airframe as, by this time, it had lost its psychological power over the enemy. The D-3 also featured an improved armor package to the undercarriage and coolant lines as a safeguard against the ever-improving Allied air defenses. Plans were made for a Ju 87D-4, a torpedo dive-bomber, but the design was ultimately scrapped. Other noteworthy variants of the Ju 87D were the D-5 and D-7. The D-5 was very similar to the D-3 but with an increased wingspan of over 15m (~45ft). The D-7 marked a significant departure from the Stuka's traditional role as a dive-bomber. In the days before the G-variant Stuka (see below) arrived on the Eastern Front, the existing Ju 87s were already undergoing trials as direct-fire, ground-attack aircraft. Therefore, Junkers developed the D-7 as a specialized night ground attack vehicle, fitted with a powerful Jumo 211P engine. A total of 3,639 D-series variants were produced by the time production ended in September 1944. Following the Ju 87D, Junkers made plans to produce an E and F series, but neither were built. Junkers instead moved on to the G variant, which fundamentally changed the Stuka's combat role.

Ju 87G

Specifications	
Crew	2
Length	11.1m
Height	3.9m
Wingspan	15m
Wing Area	33.6sq m
Tare Weight	4,400kg
Load Weight	6,600kg
Engine	Jumo 211-series, 12 cylinder
Maximum Speed	344km/h
Range	1,000km
Service Ceiling	7,320m

By 1943, the aging Stuka had been outclassed by virtually every Allied aircraft in the sky. The G variant, however, gave new life to the Stuka as a "tank buster." As the Soviets began to push the *Wehrmacht* back into Eastern Europe,

A Ju 87G on the Eastern Front, June 21, 1943. By this time, the Stuka's best days were behind it. Nevertheless, the Ju 87 performed well in the opening stages of Operation *Barbarossa* before the Soviets gained air superiority over the region. Also, during the campaign along the Eastern Front, the Stuka found a new role as a "tank buster." As shown here, many of these Stukas were retrofitted with the 3.7cm anti-tank guns. (Bundesarchiv, Bild 101I-655-5976-04)

Junkers developed the G-series to counter the growing number of Soviet armor formations. While the Ju 87G design remained virtually unchanged from its D predecessor, its power plant was updated to a Jumo 211J and given new armaments featuring two 37mm cannons. The Ju 87G also featured an improved armor package to protect the crew from the Soviets' low-altitude air defenses. The first G variants arrived at the frontline squadrons in April 1943, and saw action against the Soviets at the battle of Kursk.

Unlike its predecessors, the G-series Stuka did not have as many sub-variants. Only the G-1 and G-2 made it through the design phase. The G-1 was based on the D-3 airframe and was armed with two 37mm Flak 18 cannons, each of which were fastened under the wings outboard of the landing gear. Since the G-1 was intended to be a low-altitude aircraft, previous mission gear such as dive brakes and oxygen systems were eliminated. Identifying these non-critical systems for elimination helped compensate for the added weight of the 37mm anti-tank cannons. The G-2 differed only slightly (and almost negligibly) from its immediate predecessor. Based on the D-5 airframe, the G-2 simply removed the original MG 17 automatic machine guns. The Ju 87G was the last production variant fielded by the Luftwaffe.

D

1: Ju 87D-7
This is an example of the winter-appropriate Eastern Front colour scheme.
2: Ju 87G
A typical Ju 87G, with its anti-tank guns mounted underneath the wings.
3: Ju 87D-3
This Stuka belongs to the Romanian 1st Air Corps. During the war, Bulgaria, Romania, Hungary, Croatia, and Slovakia all operated the Stuka within their respective air forces.
4: Ju 87R
This example of the Ju 87R served with the Bulgarian air force.

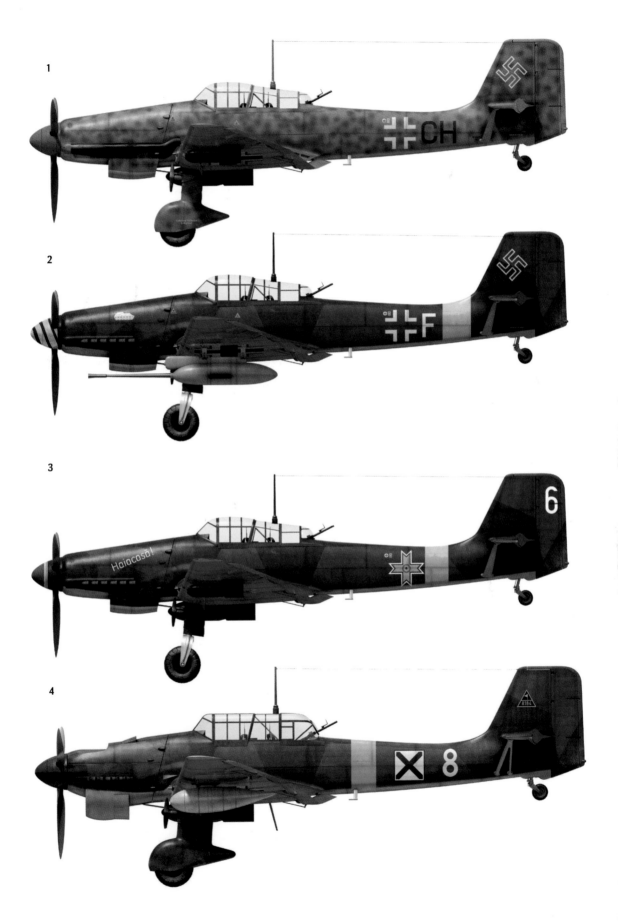

1

2

3

4

Ju 87R

Specifications	
Crew	2
Length	11.1m
Height	4.01m
Wingspan	13.6m
Wing Area	31.9sq m
Tare Weight	2,750kg
Load Weight	4,350kg
Engine	Jumo 211-series, 12 cylinder
Maximum Speed	340km/h
Range	1,800km
Service Ceiling	7,000m

A "long range" version of the Ju 87B, the R variant was designed to be an anti-shipping plane, capable of travelling longer distances to deliver bombs against enemy naval convoys. The first R variant was built on a B-series airframe. Indeed, the first R variant, R-1, was identical to the mass-produced B-1 except for the updated fuel system. Retrofitted with the same 300 liter external drop tanks used in the D-series, the Ju 87R had an extra 150 liter fuel tank installed in each wing. The Ju 87R also carried a lighter payload capacity and had a lower flight ceiling to compensate for the weight of the additional fuel. Following the development of the R-1, Junkers also produced the R-2 and R-4, which were respectively modified for operations in the Mediterranean and North Africa. The first Ju 87R units appeared over the coast of Norway during the Nazis' 1940 invasion. The R variant also appeared during the final days of Blitzkreig in France and along the Straits of Gibraltar to disrupt Allied naval convoys in the Mediterranean. A total of 972 R variants were built by the time production ended in 1941.

OPERATIONAL HISTORY

The Spanish Civil War and the Legion Condor

On July 17, 1936, the Republic of Spain erupted in a civil war. The Spanish Republican Armed Forces squared off against the Nationalists, a rebel group led by the fascist General Francisco Franco. Days after the fighting broke out, Hitler pledged Germany's support to his fellow fascists in the Iberian Peninsula.

Collectively, these German army and air units were known as the Legion Condor. Operating Germany's finest aircraft, the Legion Condor's ranks included the Heinkel He 111, Messerschmitt Bf 109, and Junkers Ju 52. However, the opportunity was ripe for the Luftwaffe to test its still-developmental Ju 87.

On the night of August 1, 1936, a single Ju 87A-0 (V4 prototype) was secretly loaded onto the German passenger ship *Usaramo* and quickly departed the port of Hamburg. To facilitate the secrecy of its shipment, this Ju 87A was given the serial number 29-1 and assigned to VJ/88, the experimental *Staffel* of the Legion Condor. After departing Germany, the *Usaramo* and its classified cargo arrived in Cadiz on August 6. In keeping with the secrecy of its deployment, very little is known today about Stuka 29-1's service in Spain.

For example, German records reveal that 29-1 was piloted by German flight officer Hermann Beuer and saw limited action at the battle of Bilbao in June 1937. The aircraft then quietly returned to Germany. Beyond these token facts, the extent of Stuka 29-1's history with the Legion Condor remains a mystery.

In January 1938, three Ju 87A-1s arrived in Vitoria, Spain. These three A-1s had come from a *Staffel* based in Barth. Carrying forward the designation of their A-0 predecessor, the trio of A-1s were given the serial numbers 29-2, 29-3, and 29-4, and were piloted, respectively, by German officers Ernst Bartels, Gerhard Weyert, and Hermann Haas. All three aircraft were incorporated into the Legion Condor's fighter wing.

The following month, the Ju 87A-1s moved to Calamocha and settled into an airfield south of Zaragoza. "And it was here," according to historian John Weal, "that the Ju 87s began to put into operational practice what up till now had only been theory." For instance, the Stuka pilots quickly discovered that the fairing-clad undercarriage of the A-1 did not mesh well with the soft, sandy soil of the Calamocha airfield. Consequently, the wheel covers were removed. Also, the Ju 87A's prescribed bomb load of 500kg could only be carried if the rear gunner's seat was empty. Subsequently, the normal bomb load was reduced to 250kg.

A *kette* of Ju 87A in picture-perfect formation. The Ju 87A served for a limited time in the Legion Condor – the *Luftwaffe*'s expeditionary air unit sent to assist the Nationalist forces during the Spanish Civil War. Note the heavily spatted landing gear. The spats were reduced on successive variants of the Stuka and, in some cases, the spats were removed entirely. (Luftwaffe RFI)

Throughout March 1938, Stukas 29-2, 29-3, and 29-4 conducted a number of dive-bomb attacks on the Spanish Republican forces as they retreated across Aragon. However, these early bombing missions – conducted by rookie pilots, operating developmental aircraft, and using experimental tactics – were not always successful. "In these early days," said Weal, "near misses nearly always outnumbered direct hits by a substantial margin, but they were learning their trade nonetheless. And as new crews from the homeland replaced the original trio on a rotational basis, a steady stream of returnees to the *Reich* were taking back with them an invaluable pool of practical experience."

Moving forward to La Cenia, the Stukas provided close air support for the rebels' attack on Valencia and the Nationalists' march to the Mediterranean Sea. However, the Republican forces launched a counter-offensive along the Ebro River in July 1938. But, in the end, this Republican counter-attack amounted to little, and the trio of Stukas scored some impressive hits on enemy troop formations south of Mequinenza. After completing many more spectacular hits on enemy shipping at Taragona and other Mediterranean ports, the Stuka A-1s returned to Germany in October 1938.

Taking their place were five Ju 87B-1s, the latest model of the Stuka series, and the first Stuka variant slated for mass production. However, by the time these B-1s arrived in Spain, the Civil War was already in its last throes. Furthermore, it seemed that their A-1 predecessors had done such a stellar job of pounding the Republicans, that there were very few pinpoint targets left to engage. Nevertheless, these Ju 87B-1s found gainful employment accompanying

A pair of Ju 87s belonging to the Legion Condor in flight over Spain. During the Spanish Civil War, the Legion Condor employed both the Ju 87A and Ju 87B variants. (Luftwaffe RFI)

the larger He 111s on their bombing runs. These five Stukas also saw action during the final weeks of the Madrid Campaign in 1939, but were unceremoniously returned to Germany before the declaration of the Nationalists' victory.

The Stuka's service in the Spanish Civil War provided an invaluable experience for its air and ground crews. Under combat conditions, these crews tested the Stuka's capabilities and made numerous modifications to the aircraft and its aerial tactics. However, the Legion Condor Stukas had operated without any serious opposition. The Luftwaffe had air superiority in the skies over Spain – and the Republicans' anti-aircraft efforts were piecemeal at best. Thus, while the Stuka pilots had full confidence in their equipment, the Ju 87 remained untested against hostile aircraft and against ground-based air defenses.

Blitzkrieg

By 1939, Hitler had set his sights on dominating Europe. Determined to right the "wrongs" which had been committed against Germany at the Treaty of Versailles, he put forth his plan to conquer the European mainland using tactics and equipment that had never been seen before. While an unsuspecting Europe remained fixated on its World War I-era military formations, the *Wehrmacht* prepared to unleash the unprecedented fury of Blitzkrieg. Spearheaded by the rapidly-deployable armor formations, and the tightly coordinated air support of the Stuka, Germany's Blitzkrieg conquered Poland, Norway, France, and the Low Countries (Belgium, Holland, and Luxembourg) within a mere ten months.

Poland

It was no coincidence that the Ju 87 was selected to carry out the first aerial attack of World War II in Europe. The easternmost province of Germany, East Prussia, was cut off from the rest of the Fatherland by the Polish Corridor.

This 19th-century drawing depicts the intricate lattice framework of the railway bridge over the Vistula River near Dirschau. The bridge was a vital terrain feature as it connected Germany proper to East Prussia through the so-called "Polish Corridor." On September 1, 1939, Polish Army sappers successfully destroyed the bridge to prevent the Germans from accessing it. (Author's collection)

"This hotly disputed strip of territory, which afforded the [otherwise] landlocked Poles access to the Baltic Sea," said Weal, "was another product of the Treaty of Versailles, and a contributory factor in Hitler's decision to attack Poland." A single railway across the Polish Corridor connected East Prussia directly to Berlin. The weakest point of the rail line was a bridge over the Vistula River near the town of Dirschau (Tczew). The Poles understood the bridge's significance – and they had preemptively rigged it with explosives, ready to detonate should the Germans ever attack. Thus, the bombing target was not the bridge itself, but the detonation site located at the nearby Dirschau station. By destroying the detonation site, Germany could prevent the Poles from destroying the bridge, and thus preserve East Prussia's lifeline to the Reich proper.

At exactly 4:26 a.m. on September 1, 1939, three Stukas from III./StG 1, led by pilot Bruno Dilly, lifted off from their air base in East Prussia en route to the Dirschau station. With their 250kg bombs attached firmly to their wings, the Stukas climbed in unison before separating, one by one, into their signature dive patterns. Within minutes, each pilot delivered his bombs with pinpoint accuracy onto the Dirschau station. Although the first dive-bomb run of World War II was a tactical success, it did not preserve the railway bridge. Undaunted, Polish Army engineers managed to destroy the bridge before the first German troop trains could arrive.

The same day, elements from I./StG 2 launched a raid on the enemy airfield at Krakow, only to find it deserted. As it turned out, most Polish Air Force units had vacated their peacetime airbases and relocated to secret, carefully secluded fields in the near countryside. After returning from their unfruitful mission at Krakow, these same Stukas spotted one of the secret airfields near Balice, just as a pair of PZL P.11c fighters were scrambling from the runway. The lead Stuka, piloted by Frank Neubert (who went on to earn the Knights Cross of the Iron Cross) shot down the P.11 piloted by Captain Mieczylaw Medwecki, making Neubert's kill the Luftwaffe's first air-to-air combat victory of World War II. According to Neubert, his shot caused the P.11 to "suddenly explode in mid-air, bursting apart like a huge fireball – the fragments literally flew around our ears."

Later on September 1, the Luftwaffe's vanguard Stukas engaged the Polish Navy at Hela in the first of several attacks on that naval base. In this engagement, four Stukas plummeted from 7,000m to attack the enemy's naval stronghold.

A *Staffel* of Stukas fly in formation over Poland during the opening days of Blitzkreig, 1939. The Stuka inaugurated Germany's aerial campaign of World War II and had a devastating effect on the Allied ground forces during the conquest of mainland Europe. (Bundesarchiv, Bild 183-1987-1210-502)

However, Hela was defended by one of the largest anti-aircraft batteries in Poland, and the diving Stukas got their first taste of enemy fire. Bracketed by the intense anti-aircraft fire, two of the four Stukas were downed by Polish guns – the first Ju 87s lost to enemy fire. Two days later, the Stukas were in action again over Gdynia, where they sank the Polish destroyer *Wicher* and the minelayer *Gryf*.

After disrupting the enemy's air and naval defenses, the Stuka could now perform its primary role in the Blitzkrieg campaign: to act as "flying artillery," disrupting the enemy ground forces and clearing a path for the oncoming Panzer and mechanized formations. Around noon on September 1, aerial reconnaissance reported a large concentration of Polish horse cavalry massing along the northern flank of the German XVI *Armeekorps* near Wielun. Major Oskar Dinort, the *Gruppenkommandeur* of I./StG 2 (and the first Stuka pilot to win the Knights Cross with Oak Leaves), recalled how his Stukas met the Polish horsemen on that fateful day:

We cross the border at a height of 2500 meters. Visibility is far from good; hardly a kilometer. Although the sun is now shining, everything is swimming in an opalescent haze. Suddenly a group of buildings – either a large estate or a small village. Smoke is already rising. Wielun – the target!

I stuff my map away, set the sights, close the radiator flaps; do all those things we've already done a hundred times or more in practice, but never with a feeling so intense as today. Then bank slightly, drop the left wing and commence the dive. The air brakes screech, all the blood in my body is forced downwards. 1200 meters – press the bomb release. A tremor runs through the machine. The first bomb is on its way.

Recover – bank – corkscrew – and then a quick glance below. Bang on target, a direct hit on the road. The black snake of men and horses that had been crawling along it has now come to a complete standstill. Now for that large estate, packed with men and wagons. Our height scarcely 1200 meters, we dive to 800. Bombs away! The whole lot goes up in smoke and flames.

By mid-afternoon, the *Wehrmacht* confirmed that as a farm complex just north of Wielun housed the entire headquarters of the Polish *Wolynska* brigade. In response, 60 Ju 87s belonging to the I and II./StG 77 destroyed the headquarters outpost and the Germans occupied Wielan that night.

In the following days, the Stuka squadrons performed over 300 bombing runs on civilian and military targets as the *Wehrmacht* sped towards the Polish capital, Warsaw. In the European tradition of conventional warfare, it was understood that once the enemy's capital had fallen, the game was over. The Poles obviously understood this as well as the Germans did. Indeed, the 24 infantry brigades and six mounted brigades defending Polish borderlands put every ounce of strength they had into preventing the Nazis from reaching Warsaw. Yet, Poland's defenses gradually eroded under the relentless bombardment (and the terrifying wails) of the Stuka dive-bomber.

As the Poles retreated towards Warsaw, however, many of their number invariably became separated from the main retreat. One such contingent included six Polish divisions that were trapped between Radom and their fallback point near the Vistula River. As the Panzer forces surrounded the beleaguered Poles, more than 150 Stukas arrived overhead to pound the enemy troops into submission. After four days of enduring the relentless 50kg fragmentation bombs, and hearing the dreadful scream of the Jericho Trumpet, the encircled Polish units finally gave up.

A few days later, the Stukas participated in the battle of Bzura. The Polish *Poznan* Army (consisting of four infantry divisions and two cavalry brigades) had moved southeast across the Bzura River, trying to reach the Vistula in attempt to break through the frontline screen of the German 8.*Armee*. The ensuing battle of Bzura, which was essentially an "air-versus-ground engagement," effectively broke the back of the remaining Polish resistance. During this battle alone, the Stukas dropped over 388 metric tons of ordnance on the beleaguered Polish defenders.

Following the collapse of Poland's defenses, the Stuka units turned their attention to Warsaw proper. The enemy capital, however, with its few remaining air defense batteries, put up a valiant last stand against the invading Stukas and other Luftwaffe aircraft. In fact, one Ju 87 pilot recalled how tight the Polish defenses were around the capital city:

I had just recovered from the dive and was corkscrewing back up to altitude when the Polish 40mm flak caught me fair and square in its crossfire. The 'red tomatoes' which

Three Stukas take flight from a German-occupied airfield on another bombing mission over Poland. (Bundesarchiv, Bild 101I-318-0053-35)

this dangerous weapon spewed out were flying around my ears. Suddenly there was an almighty crash in the machine. There I was, 1200 meters over the middle of Warsaw, and I could immediately tell that the machine was no longer maneuverable.

My gunner reported that the elevator had been shot off and there were only a few scraps left fluttering in the wind. Quick decision: the airfield just south of Warsaw was already in German hands…I had to make it. The machine was steadily losing height, but I slowly coaxed it along, gently slide-slipped and got safely down on the first attempt.

But despite the Poles' best efforts against the Luftwaffe, the air defenses around the city eventually collapsed. Warsaw fell to the Germans on September 27, 1939 – less than one month after the start of the invasion. Throughout the campaign, only 31 Stukas had been lost to enemy fire.

Norway

After pacifying Poland, Hitler turned his attention to Norway. His decision to invade the westernmost country of Scandinavia was based on its relative position to the *Reich*. Hitler needed a coastal safeguard against an Allied invasion and a territorial buffer to protect Germany's steady stream of iron ore imported from Sweden. However, the narrow and mountainous terrain in Norway ruled out the possibility of using the Stuka-Panzer integration tactics that had been so critical in taking Poland. Instead, the Nazis relied heavily on airborne insertions and ski-equipped troops.

The only Stuka unit to partake in the Norwegian campaign was I./StG 1 which, following the Polish campaign, had been refitted with the Ju 87R. Nevertheless, I./StG 1 proved highly effective in its ground-attack and anti-shipping role against the Norwegians.

The operation to take Norway, known as Operation *Weserübung*, began on April 9, 1940.[2] At 10:59 a.m., 22 Ju 87Ds took flight from German-occupied airfields to destroy the Oscarsborg Fortress. The Norwegian defenders had sunk the German battle cruiser *Blücher*, which had disrupted the amphibious landings along the fjord-laden coastline. Although the Ju 87Ds hit the fortress hard, their attack was of little consequence; Oscarsborg did not surrender until after Oslo fell to the Nazis.

Returning to the airfield, the Stukas of StG 1 were airborne again later that day, whereupon they encountered the Norwegian destroyer *Aeger*. Barrelling into their dives, these Stukas succeeded in hitting the engine room, which gave the destroyer's captain just enough time to run the ship aground and scuttle her before she fell into enemy hands. Further into the campaign, the Stuka also scored some impressive victories against the Royal Navy. Within one week, the HMS *Bittern* and HMS *Afridi* had been lost to the Stukas' bombardment. In between these two victories against

---

2   As almost a minor adjunct, Germany invaded Denmark the same day. The Danes capitulated within 24 hours.

E   A Ju 87B in a dive over Poland in the opening days of Blitzkreig. Note the fixed landing gear and inverted gull wings. The inverted wings allowed the flight crew to have better observation of the situation on the ground. The Ju 87 spearheaded the air campaign over Poland, Norway, France, and the Low Countries. Although the Stuka was widely feared throughout Europe, its reputation was inflated because the Allies had yet to gain air superiority over the continent. However, once the Ju 87 went up against the RAF during the Battle of Britain, its fearsome reputation fell by the wayside.

After conquering Norway and Denmark, the Nazis turned their attention towards France and the Low Countries. Here, a Stuka from StG 2 rests in a temporary assembly area near St Trond in Belgium. (Luftwaffe RFI)

His Majesty's fleet, the resident Stukas also succeeded in attacking the French super-destroyer *Bison*. Sending a direct hit into her forward magazine compartment, the Stukas' bombs killed 108 of the *Bison's* crew and rendered the ship inoperable.

With the fighting in central Norway drawing to a close, the Luftwaffe set its sight on the last remaining Allied stronghold on the Scandinavian Peninsula: Narvik. A thriving port city, Narvik was an important outlet to the sea for Norwegian iron ores. Moving up the peninsula to Mosjöen on May 24, I./StG 1 sank a Norwegian trawler in Bodo harbor. The engagement, however, resulted in the loss of one Stuka, shot down by a British Gladiator II belonging to No 263 Sqn – "one of three detached to Bodo to protect retreating British troops in the area."

In June 1940, the Luftwaffe launched its culminating attacks on Narvik. Three Ju 87s were lost during that time. The first two aerial losses occurred during the second wave of the attack on Narvik. Both Stukas crashed following engagements with British Hawker Hurricane fighters from No 46 Sqn. The third Stuka went down during the final wave. Piloted by Heinz Böhme (who had achieved an admirable flight record in the Mediterranean theatre), this ill-fated Ju 87 was one of a pair being trailed by two Gladiator II fighters. Böhme's Stuka was already in bad shape: one of his under-wing fuel tanks was engulfed in flames. While the other Stuka trailed off into the clouds and lived to fight another day, Böhme's plane was last seen headed into the mountains, where he crashed and died. Meanwhile, on the French shores of the English Channel, the British Army had just made its escape from Dunkirk. But as the beleaguered Brits fled across the channel, France and the Low Countries fell into the merciless orbit of Nazi Germany.

France and the Low Countries

The Stukas tapped for the final conquest of mainland Europe spent March and April 1940 practicing their maneuvers and flight formations. Finally, on May 10, 1940, a wave of Ju 87s from StG 2 set a course for the Belgian fortress of Eben Emael. The fortress was a critical threat as it was the only feature in Belgium that could have presented a challenge to the German advance. The fortress was barely five years old and had an impressive array of concrete casemates, steel cupolas, and anti-aircraft batteries. Dominating the countryside, Eben Emael's guns covered the Dutch border town of Maastricht and three bridges which the Axis considered to be vital crossing points in their invasion of the Low Countries. If the Belgian fortress remained standing, and its guns intact, the campaign for the Low Countries would likely fall apart. Fortunately for the Luftwaffe, a contingent of German airborne troops had stormed Eben Emael and disabled its guns before the Stukas arrived. Nevertheless, StG 2 inflicted considerable damage upon the fort's peripheral defenses. Meanwhile, StG 77 took flight from Cologne-Butzweilerhof to attack enemy positions along the River Meuse near Liège. Later that evening, StG 2 and StG 77 combined their efforts for a dive-bomb attack on Antwerp.

However, it was during this campaign in the Low Countries when the Stuka's vulnerabilities were first brought to light – poor maneuverability, slow airspeed, and the lack of adequate armor or defensive armaments. On the first day of the operation, the Luftwaffe lost more than a dozen Stukas, all from anti-aircraft fire. The following day, six Ju 87s from StG 2 were downed after they came under attack from a posse of Hawker Hurricanes belonging to the RAF's No 87 Squadron.

Still, with Belgian forces on the ropes, the Ju 87s continued their bombing campaign. Moving west towards Bierset, the Stukas from StG 77 set their sights on Fort Flémalle. Although Flémalle was arguably not as troublesome as Eben Emael, this countryside fortress had disrupted the *Wehrmacht*'s ground advance. Hence, it wasn't long before the Stukas of StG 77 went airborne to neutralize the offending fort. The bombardment that followed was a picture-perfect example of the Stuka's destructive power when unopposed from the air. Although the fort was effectively de-fanged, it did not surrender until May 17.

Soon after the fall of Flémalle, the German offensive burst through the Ardennes and sped towards the Meuse River crossing point at the town of Sedan. Once the Axis advance had cleared that crossing point, they would have unrestricted access to the coast along the English Channel. On May 13, StG 77 sent their Stukas on more than 200 sorties. Together with the onslaught of the Panzer forces and the hail of artillery, the wailing Stukas broke the backs of the French defenders. Barely two days later, the German Army crossed the River Meuse.

Dashing into the French countryside beyond the Meuse, the Stuka and Panzer forces continued their onslaught against what remained of the Allied resistance. These coordinated dive-bomb attacks succeeded in breaking up the enemy's armored counterattacks. Maintaining their synchronization with the Panzers, the Ju 87s flew in front of the armored formations to clear any pockets of resistance ahead of the main advance. And to keep pace with their Panzer brethren, the Stukas leap-frogged across the countryside, establishing temporary airfields upon any flat piece of terrain they could find. Around this time, the frontline Stuka units received the first batch of Ju 87Rs, which

Soldiers of the British Expeditionary Force awaiting evacuation at Dunkirk, 1940. During the invasion of France, the battered British forces retreated to the shores of the English Channel, where they narrowly escaped aboard a flotilla of naval, commercial, and privately-owned vessels. Many of the retreating units, however, fell victim to the Stukas' bombardment. (Imperial War Museum HU 1137)

provided a greater boost to their operational endurance (these units had previously been equipped with the shorter-ranged Ju 87B).

By May 21, the British, Belgian, and elements of the French Army had been isolated with their backs to the sea at Dunkirk. Meanwhile, the Stukas of StG 2 and StG 77 pounded away at the Anglo-French perimeter near Dunkirk. Elsewhere along the Channel coast, one French port after another fell to the *Wehrmacht* – Boulogne was occupied on May 25 following heavy bombardment from the local Stukas. The following day, Allied forces at Calais surrendered after an intense bombardment from StG 2 and StG 77.

In what was perhaps the greatest escape in military history, a hodge-podge flotilla of nearly 1,000 vessels (including tugboats, merchant ships, private yachts, passenger liners, and Royal Navy craft) left the shores of Britain to rescue the stranded Allied forces at Dunkirk. This motley assortment of boats began evacuating the British Expeditionary Force during the final days of May. Unfortunately for the Luftwaffe, rain and heavy cloud cover near Dunkirk had grounded all Stuka missions until at least May 29. The Stukas may have succeeded in destroying the evacuation force had it not been for the weather. When the cloud cover finally lifted, however, the Stukas did succeed in sinking the HMS *Grenade* and several privately-owned vessels. Bad weather kept the Stukas grounded for another two days but they returned to the skies on June 1 in a bombing campaign that lasted all day. One lucky pilot landed his bomb straight down the aft funnel of HMS *Keith*, one of three Royal Navy destroyers sunk that day.

Despite this aerial bombardment, however, the hastily-assembled fleet succeeded in evacuating 338,226 troops (198,229 British and 139,997 French) from the shores of Dunkirk. The mostly-French rearguard force, who had been protecting the evacuation from the ground, formally surrendered on June 4.

All told, Dunkirk had been a success for the British. For the French, however, their situation was about to get much worse.

Over the next two weeks, the Germans initiated Operation *Red*, the second phase of their invasion. Now that the Low Countries and northern France had been pacified, it was time to close in on central France. As the French retreated across the Somme River, the attendant Stukas remained on standby to disrupt any counterattacks and destroy key bridges to delay the French Army's retreat. On June 7, a German war correspondent flying aboard a Stuka gave the following account:

> Yesterday, we were over one of the main assembly points for enemy troops – a town some ten minutes flying time east of Paris, which was just visible through the layer of smoke and haze which covers every large city. Otherwise, the sky was as bright and cloudless as only a summer sky can be. We sat under the glass canopy of the cockpit as if in some flying greenhouse, suffering the full effect of the sun. You could feel the sweat trickling down your back under the one-piece flying overalls and beading your forehead below the tightly fitting helmet. A few small specks in the distance were our fighter escort. [We] kept in tight formation as we approached the target. Others flew to the left and right of us.
>
> 'Fasten your harness, we're diving!' the pilot called out. It was almost as if – for a split second – the machine hung motionless in the sky. Then the tail rose almost vertically as the nose tipped earthwards. The flow of the air built up, whistling over the wing surfaces and beating against the cabin windows. The ground – a moment ago a relief model unfolding below us with contours, hills, and a horizon – was suddenly a flat map filling our entire field of vision.
>
> The pilot hung motionless in his seat, his right eye pressed against the sight as he concentrated on the target. The howl of the engine rose and drowned the noise of the wind. There's the bridge! His finger pressed the button on the control column marked with the word 'Bombs.'
>
> At almost the same moment I was pressed down hard in my seat as the pilot began to pull out. I swallowed to relieve the pressure in my ears. The wings flexed slightly. Then we were flying horizontally, but jinking to the left and right, rising and falling, to throw the enemy flak gunners off their aim as we reformed for the for the homeward flight.

On June 12, the Germans crossed the Marne, and Paris was declared an open city the following day. The Stukas from StG 2 and StG 77 continued to encounter pockets of resistance and a few French fighter aircraft in the run up to Paris. However, just a few days later, Marshal Pétain formally surrendered to the Nazis and signed an armistice with Germany, dividing France into unoccupied and occupied zones. Throughout the campaign in the France and the Low Countries, the Luftwaffe lost 120 Stukas. Unbeknownst to the Germans, however, the Stuka's heyday was about to come to an abrupt end.

The Battle of Britain

With mainland Europe firmly within the Axis' orbit, Hitler cast his eyes toward the British Isles. To this end, Hitler issued Directive No. 16 to the *Wehrmacht* – ordering the preparations for an aerial attack on Britain to clear the way for an amphibious invasion. According to Hitler and the Nazi high command, the invasion of Britain (Operation *Sea Lion*) would be successful only if the Luftwaffe achieved air superiority over the British Isles.

Ju 87s lift off on a mission to conquer the British Isles. With the European mainland firmly under Axis control, Hitler expected to make short work of the Royal Air Force before invading Great Britain. However, these aerial skirmishes finally revealed the Stuka's weaknesses. In fact, the Ju 87 fared poorly when pitted against the RAF fighter units. During and after the Battle of Britain, the Stuka could only operate effectively when accompanied by a fighter escort. (Luftwaffe RFI)

During the early days of the Battle of Britain, the Stuka proved to be a remarkable anti-shipping weapon. July 4, 1940 became one of the deadliest days for the Royal Navy in their struggle against the Luftwaffe. For on that day, StG 2 successfully sunk four destroyers in the English Channel: the HMS *Britsum*, *Dallas City*, *Deucalion* and *Kolga*. Later that afternoon, some 33 Ju 87s evaded the local RAF patrols and sank the HMS *Foylebank* at Portland Harbour, killing 176 of its 298 crewmen. Only one Stuka was lost during the raid on the *Foylebank* and, although the cause of its demise remains unknown, it was likely downed by Leading Seaman JF Mantle. Mantle became a hero in British naval history on that day when, despite being mortally wounded, he stayed at his post and continued to fire on the diving Stukas even as the ship sank beneath the waves.

The Stukas' early success continued into August as the Luftwaffe reached the RAF bases on the British mainland. On August 13, 1940, the Germans launched a coordinated attack on the RAF Fighter Command's network of airbases, in what became known as *Aldertag* (Eagle Day). During a wave of the *Aldertag* attacks, a contingent of Messerschmitt Bf 109s flew ahead of the main force to lure away the RAF fighters and give the 86 Ju 87s from StG 1 an unobstructed path to destroy the RAF airbase at Detling. This operation exemplified Stuka-fighter integration for the remainder of the campaign. Now that the Ju 87 was facing a stiff and highly-organized air resistance, its fighter escorts became even more essential.

Although the attack on RAF Detling was a success, it did little to help the Luftwaffe's air campaign – Detling, as it turned out, was not an RAF Fighter Command base. Meanwhile, StG 77 (also under Bf 109 escort) went out in search of RAF Warmwell. Although the Stukas found no opposition in the air, they could not find their intended target either. Thus, not wanting to put their sortie to waste, they began dropping their bombs at random over the Dorset countryside. Indeed, many of the Ju 87 sorties were muddled by poor intelligence and communication.

On August 16, however, the Stukas did succeed in executing a textbook attack on the RAF fighter station at Tangmere. Although most of the base's fighters had been scrambled, they were unable to stop the Ju 87s from delivering their ordnance with the usual pinpoint accuracy. Still, the defending fighters (Supermarine Spitfires and Hawker Hurricanes) intercepted the Stukas at their most vulnerable – while recovering from their dive patterns. Historian John Weal recalls that Tangmere had been a "salutary lesson." Indeed, the lack of any organized, effective fighter opposition "had ill-prepared the Stuka's supporters within the Luftwaffe High Command for the losses which their much-vaunted 'flying artillery' was now beginning to suffer in its new, longer-range, role. Even its staunchest advocates were having to concede that the Stuka was not operable as a strategic weapon if pitted against a determined defense." During the skirmish at Tangmere, the Spitfires had been able to keep the Bf 109 escorts busy while the Hurricanes made short work of the unguarded Stukas. Tangmere, as it were, was the beginning of the end for the Stuka's career in Western Europe. "It would take just one more reversal," said Weal "to write *finis* to its career in the west."

That reversal came on August 18, 1940, in what became known as the Hardest Day. On that aptly named day, the Luftwaffe returned to Britain in full fury to destroy the RAF Fighter Command. Aerial reconnaissance identified four priority targets: RAF airfields at Ford, Thorney Island, Gosport, and the radar station at Poling in West Sussex. Luftwaffe intelligence had mistakenly identified these airfields as fighter stations; the high altitude of the reconnaissance missions and the poor resolution of the photographs had led them to believe that the airfields were home to various fighter squadrons. In reality, however, none of the observed airfields belonged to RAF Fighter Command: Ford was a naval air station; Thorney Island belonged to the No. 59 and 235 Squadrons (both of which were bomber units); and Gosport was home to a torpedo development unit. For the attack, the three *Stukagruppen* of StG 77 committed 109 Ju 87s – the largest concentration of Stukas yet seen over Britain. The 28 Stukas from I./StG 77, were assigned to destroy Thorney Island. The II and III./StG 77 Stukas were to destroy Ford and the Poling radar station, respectively. Meanwhile, 22 Stukas from StG 3 were designated to attack Gosport. The Ju 87s' fighter escort consisted of more than 150 Bf 109s, some of which were tasked to fly ahead of the main advance and clear the area surrounding Portsmouth. On the morning of the attack, the Stukas staged at the occupied airfields outside Cherbourg, right along the coast of the English Channel. Once there, each Ju 87 received a full bomb load and its fuel tanks were filled to capacity.

After the crews had received their final briefings, the first Ju 87s took off at 1:29 p.m. By 1:45, all were in formation and flying the first leg of their 85-mile trip. Most of their Bf 109 fighter escort remained behind; they would not take off until later in the day. The distance to the target, coupled with the low airspeed of the Ju 87s, allowed the Bf 109s enough time to catch up to the formation en route to Portsmouth. This in turn would allow the Bf 109s to conserve fuel for the dogfights that were sure to follow their arrival over Britain.

Meanwhile, across the English Channel, the radar station at Poling picked up the German formations at 1:59 p.m., reporting them as 80-strong.

In this iconic photograph, a crippled Stuka dives to its doom, shot down on August 18, 1940 near Chichester, England. The Luftwaffe suffered tremendous losses during the Battle of Britain, losing more than 60 Stukas and ultimately failing to conquer the British Isles. (Royal Air Force)

However it was an underestimation by more than half. Upon receiving word of the incoming German attack, the RAF No. 10 Group scrambled their squadrons at RAF Middle Wallop, Exeter and Warmwell, while No. 11 Group dispatched its units from Tangmere and Westhampnett. This flying armada included some 34 Spitfires and 21 Hurricanes – plus 12 more Spitfires waiting in reserve near Middle Wallop.

Although the British were outnumbered by a ratio of nearly four to one (accounting for both German fighters *and* bombers), they fought valiantly throughout the skirmish. The enemy Bf 109s that were part of the pre-attack clearing missions were intercepted by fighters from No. 266 Squadron and, despite a grueling dogfight, lost only two Spitfires, one Hurricane, with six Hurricanes damaged but salvageable.

As the Ju 87s reached the Channel coast, the flight groups split off and headed for their respective targets. By this time, the Bf 109 fighter escort had caught up to the Stukas and had assumed their defensive positions around the dive-bombers. Helmut Bode, the celebrated commander of III./StG 77, led his *Gruppen* to attack from the northwest, into the direction of the wind in order to bomb more accurately. Usually, the Ju 87 formations attacked in line astern, but Bode chose to keep his Stukas in groups of three to split up the enemy's anti-aircraft fire. Taking the Ju 87 into its signature dive, Bode fired the Stuka's cannons while the plane plummeted at 80 degree angle. Diving from an altitude of 13,000ft, Bode dropped his ordnance on the Poling radar station before pulling out at 2,275ft.

The radar station at Poling suffered heavy damage from the Stuka bombardment. In fact, Poling had taken so much punishment that it remained out of commission until September. Fortunately for the British, there was another functioning radar station on the Isle of Wight, which effectively kept tabs on German air movements for the rest of the campaign. Meanwhile, II/StG 77, commanded by Alfons Orthofer, pounded away at Ford. With only six anti-aircraft guns guarding the base, the Ju 87s made quick work of the airfield. The hangars, oil tanks, and many of the grounded aircraft went up in flames as the Stukas crippled the RAF station. Gosport suffered a similar fate as StG 3 attacked with no aerial opposition.

While most of the Stuka groups reached their targets without incident, I./StG 77 with its 28 Stukas were intercepted by a force of 18 Hawker Hurricanes from the No. 43 and No. 601 Squadrons. The escorting Bf 109s were too far away to stop the Hurricanes before they fired on the Ju 87s. During the ensuing melee, three Stukas were shot down and one Hurricane damaged by return fire. As the Bf 109s caught up to the Stuka formation, they too came under attack, rendering their escort duty effectively useless. Still, some of the Ju 87s were able to deliver their bombs. By this time, however, the local RAF squadrons were out in full force: No. 152 and 253 Squadrons engaged the Germans over Thorney Island while No. 602 engaged the Stukas that attacked Ford.

These air battles cost the *Stukagruppen* heavily. I./StG 77 lost ten Stukas while II./StG 77 lost three of their number to enemy fire and one damaged beyond repair. III./StG 77 also lost two Ju 87s and had two more damaged. All told, the Luftwaffe lost 59 Stukas in the air battles over Britain with an additional 33 damaged. Soon thereafter, Germany concluded that the cost of sending the Stukas over the English Channel was too high and, notwithstanding a few token raids on shipping convoys, the Stuka played no further part in the Battle of Britain.

Service in the *Regia Aeronautica* (Italian Air Force)

Fascist Italy was the first Axis partner to receive a large export of Ju 87s. The Italians had developed their own dive-bomber in the late 1930s: the Savoia-Marchetti SM.85. Dubbed the "Flying Banana" because of the airframe's curvature, this experimental dive-bomber was a dismal failure. Its only sortie ended after many fruitless hours of searching for a British naval convoy reported off the coast of Malta. To make matters worse, the wooden structures of the SM.85 did not mesh well with the Mediterranean summers – the heat and humidity left the airframes badly warped.

Still, Mussolini remained convinced that the *Regia Aeronautica* needed a dive-bomber. To that end, he solicited help from Nazi Germany, whereupon General Pricolo, Chief of the Italian Air Staff, negotiated the purchase of enough Ju 87s to equip two bomber *gruppi*. Consequently, by the fall of 1940, the *Regia Aeronautica* had sent over two dozen of its pilots to the Luftwaffe's Stuka-Schule 2 at Graz-Thalerhof, Austria. Each Italian pilot who enrolled in the course received an accelerated course in German avionics and the Stuka's handling. Because most of the students were former fighter pilots, they were quick to learn and the valued the Stuka as a remarkable improvement from their disastrous SM.85.

The first Ju 87s delivered to Italy were extracted directly from the Luftwaffe and simply had their Iron Crosses and swastikas painted over with Italian roundels. The Italians also re-branded their Stuka as the "Picchiatello," which meant "slightly crazy" but was also a pun of sorts on the aeronautical term "picchiata" – an aerial dive. But despite its makeover and the new name, the Italian Stuka would never achieve the notoriety of its German counterparts.

Italian pilots with the *Regia Aeronautica* pose in front an Italian Ju 87. Nazi Germany supplied several Stukas to Mussolini's air force and even trained many of the Italian pilots at *Luftwaffe* flight schools. The Italians gave the Ju 87 the nickname "Picchiatello" – a double-entendre of sorts. In aeronautical terms, the word "Picchiatello" conveyed a diving maneuver; however, in colloquial Italian, it also meant "slightly crazy." (Riccardo Nicola)

Several weeks after the inaugural flight of the SM.85, the *Regia Aeronautica*'s 96° *Gruppo* (with their 15 Stukas) engaged the British aircraft carrier *Illustrious* off the coast of Malta. The ensuing battle, however, did not yield any significant gains for either side. The attacking aircraft reported hitting two Royal Navy ships, while the defenders claimed to have shot down five Italian Stukas. Two days later, five Ju 87s from 96° *Gruppo* performed the first dive-bomb raid on Malta, raining their bombs on Fort Delimara.

The raids continued throughout August and into September. On September 17, 96° *Gruppo* returned to Malta, this time targeting the Luqa airfield. The bombing raid was itself was a textbook operation but it cost the 96° their first combat casualties: one of their Ju 87s was shot down by a Hawker Hurricane while another returned to the airfield with a dead gunner aboard. But the raid of September 17 was 96° *Gruppo*'s last sortie over Malta. By October 1940, Mussolini had set his sights elsewhere. Having already invaded Albania, *il Duce* now set out to conquer Greece.

To support the invasion of Greece, Mussolini staged his troops and elements of the *Regia Aeronautica* along the Albanian border. Among the aerial units covering the ground invasion was 96° *Gruppo*, flying both the Ju 87B and R configurations. Although the opening days of the invasion went well for the Italians, the Greeks soon launched a fierce counteroffensive which drove the Italian Army back across the Albanian border towards the town of Koritza, the forwardmost logistics base of Mussolini's forces. In response, 96° *Gruppo* mounted their first raids against the Greek Army on November 2: six Ju 87Bs attacked Corfu and five Ju 87Rs dropped their bombs farther inland at Yannina. Despite this strong air support, however, Mussolini's troops continued their retreat, and Koritza fell to the Greeks on November 23, 1940.

Meanwhile, the *Regia Aeronautica* activated its second, fully-functioning Stuka unit: the 97° *Gruppo*. They carried out their first mission on November 28: a failed attack on the HMS *Glasgow* and her attendant Royal Navy destroyers off the coast of Malta. However, they were soon diverted to assist the stalled campaign in Albania. As it turned out, the Italians' offensive in the lower Balkans was quickly falling apart. The Greek counterattack had pushed Mussolini's forces back even farther: now into the Albanian towns of Argyrokastron and Santi Quaranta. On December 14, the newly-minted 97° *Gruppo* carried out its mission against the Greeks, targeting enemy positions along the coastal road near Corfu. Five days later, 96° *Gruppo* took to the skies over Santi Quarana, dive-bombing in picture perfect formation and claiming the loss of one enemy vessel moored in the harbor. The 96° *Gruppo* returned to action on December 21, attacking Greek positions farther inland along the mountains.

Still, Mussolini found himself unable to reverse the tides of his misadventure in the Balkans. Desperate for relief, he once again turned to Adolf Hitler for help. The Luftwaffe responded by diverting several of its Ju 52 transports to enhance the Italian

Some captured Ju 87s found their way into the ranks of the RAF. This Stuka, once belonging to the *Regia Aeronautica*, was abandoned by its Italian crew after running out of fuel. Rebranded with the RAF roundels, this captured Stuka remained in service with the RAF until 1944, when wing corrosion forced its retirement. (Australian War Museum)

Army's supply lines across the Adriatic. Meanwhile, the Greeks solicited help from the British. Although the RAF certainly had its hands full defending the skies over Britain, Prime Minister Churchill was not about to let another country fall into the Axis orbit. The British Army hastily sent troops to the Greek mainland and select RAF squadrons fell in alongside the Greek Air Force.

Responding to the increased British presence in the Mediterranean, Italy intensified its air power in Sicily. With 97° *Gruppo* carrying on in Albania, 96° *Gruppo* relocated to its erstwhile airbase at Comiso to interdict any more incoming Allied convoys to Greece or other Axis territory. Although 96° *Gruppo*'s pilots performed admirably against the targets they engaged, the Ju 87 Picchiatello operations were little more than pinpricks when compared to their German counterparts.

Meanwhile, 97° *Gruppo* carried on against the Greeks in Albania. Throughout the opening months of 1941, the *Gruppo* lost several Ju 87s to anti-aircraft fire. Undaunted, the Italian Ju 87s continued their raids across the Straits of Otranto. During this time, one of 97° *Gruppo*'s senior pilots, Capitano Guiseppe Cenni, developed an innovative way of attacking Allied naval convoys. Realizing that the Ju 87 would never be available to the *Regia Aeronautica* in quantities sufficient to duplicate the Luftwaffe's success in Blitzkrieg, Cenni devised an ingeniously economical way of sinking enemy ships – opting for a shallow dive and leveling the plane into a horizontal flight path just above the surface of the water, but below the gun line of the ship's armament. Cenni would then release the bomb and its forward momentum would cause it to bounce across the surface of the water (much like a stone skipping across a pond) before smashing into the ship's hull.

The "Cenni Method," as it was known, successfully destroyed the Greek freighter *Susanna* and the Greek naval vessel *Poussa*. But these victories represented the last of the Picchiatello's solo reign in the Mediterranean. For less than two days after the sinking of the *Poussa*, Hitler invaded the Balkans, taking the brunt of the fighting off Mussolini's stagnated forces.

Luftwaffe operations in the Mediterranean: Yugoslavia, Greece, and Crete

Reluctantly, Hitler came to Mussolini's rescue in Greece and in the Balkans. The *Führer* had already driven the British from mainland Europe four months earlier at Dunkirk; he hardly looked forward to fending off another British Expeditionary Force in the Mediterranean. Also, with his pending plan to invade the Soviet Union, the very last thing Hitler wanted was to get bogged down in a sideshow along the Adriatic Sea. Still, Hitler was confident that he could drive the British from the region. He boasted that "they retreated quickly enough the last time we let our Panzers and Stukas loose on them. No doubt they'll do the same again!"

To help his comrade-in-arms, Hitler had intended to invade only Greece. However, political unrest in Yugoslavia soon brought that nation into the Reich's crosshairs. In March 1941, Yugoslavia became a signator to the Axis' Tripartite Pact but, less than two days after signing on to Hitler's camp, a swift coup deposed the reign of Prince Paul and proclaimed Peter Karadordevic the new King of Yugoslavia. Suddenly, the new regime declared its neutrality and sought to remove itself from any of the Axis' dealings on the continent. Infuriated, Hitler expanded his Greek expedition into Yugoslavia.

Stukas from I./StG 3 in flight over Yugoslavia, 1941. After Germany failed to conquer the British Isles in 1940, Hitler diverted his Stukas to the Mediterranean. In this theater, the Ju 87 assisted Mussolini when the latter's invasion of Greece backfired. Almost simultaneously, the Stukas participated in the invasion of Yugoslavia and the naval battles against Greek and British Commonwealth forces. (Luftwaffe RFI)

In the spring of 1941, elements of StG 2, StG 3, and StG 77 all began staging for operations in Yugoslavia. Sensing the imminent hostilities, the Yugoslav government declared Belgrade an "open city" on April 3, 1941. But Hitler, furious that Yugoslavia had dared to defy him, would have none of it – he ordered a full-scale assault on the capital city. The ground invasion began on April 6, 1941 when German troops crossed the Bulgarian border. At 7:00 a.m. that same morning, the Luftwaffe began its saturation bombing of Belgrade. Flying from airfields in Austria and Romania, the first wave of bombers over the city included seventy-five Stukas from StG 77. Just as they had done over Norway and Poland, the Ju 87s delivered their bombs with a pinpoint accuracy, crumbling the city's landmarks within minutes. One Stuka pilot recounted his assault on the city as such:

> The morning sun was glinting off the peaks of the Translyvanian Alps at our backs as we approached the unmistakable silvery ribbon of the Danube, the frontier between Romania and Yugoslavia. The hazy outlines of a large city appeared in the distance – Belgrade!
>
> Below us the first few bursts of enemy flak. But nothing to worry about. Those of us who'd been through Poland and France had seen much worse. The city was much clearer now. The white tower-like apartment blocks bright in the morning sun. Our target was the fortress which gave the city its name. Perched high above the promontory where the Sava joins the Danube, it could not be missed.
>
> I felt the jolt as our bomb was released. We levelled out and turned back for base at high speed, ready to prepare for the next mission. As we retired I saw the fortress ringed in smoke and flames. Fires had also been started in the royal palace and the nearby main railway station. Soon smoke hung over the whole city like a grey shroud.

While the bombardment of Belgrade continued over the next several days, StG 77 was soon diverted to conduct bombing raids on various Yugoslav air bases and other military targets.

Meanwhile, farther south, StG 2 supported the Panzers' armored strike into the Yugoslav countryside. By attacking through the southeastern border with Bulgaria, the *Wehrmacht* hope to take the Royal Yugoslav armed forces by surprise and drive a wedge between them and the Greeks to the south. StG 2 took flight ahead of the Panzer formations to knock out the Yugoslav

The bombing of Belgrade, 1941. A reluctant ally of the Third Reich, Yugoslavia suffered an internal coup which ousted the pro-Nazi government. Hitler responded by bombing Belgrade into submission. StG 77 saw extensive action over the city. (*Der Alder* Magazine, April 1941)

military outposts guarding the mountain passes near the Bulgarian borderlands. Watching from his mount, a German tank gunner recalled the action of the sorties overhead:

> Despite the racket, my ears picked up the thin drone of aircraft engines, growing louder by the second. I knew from experience what it was, and pointed the glasses [binoculars] upwards. Sure enough, the dim shapes of approaching Stukas. Now they were circling above us, the dark red pinpoints of their position lights plainly visible beneath the shadows of their wings.
>
> They slowly began to climb, breaking into the clear light of the new day. More and more aircraft joined them as they headed towards the ridge of the mountains immediately to our front. One last circle, as if to make doubly sure of the target below, and then the first [Stukas] went into their dives. Even from here we could hear the familiar nerve-shattering howl of their sirens. And then the first bombs fell. The tiny black specks rained down on the enemy's positions. The noise of the explosions echoed back from unseen clefts in the mountains…pillars of yellow-brown smoke were staining the pristine whiteness of the high snowfields.

With these systematic air raids, the pilots of StG 2 cleared the way for the Panzers to storm across the Yugoslav countryside. After Skoplje and Nis fell, the Axis war machine finally closed in on Belgrade. Beset by enemy forces on all sides, Yugoslavia surrendered on April 17, 1941. However, even before the fall of Belgrade, the Luftwaffe had already begun diverting their forces southwards to Greece. The British contingent in Greece had already begun their retreat and Hermann Göring was determined to crush them before they could escape to sea.

Capturing Greece, however, would prove to be no easy task. Just as in Yugoslavia, the Greek borderlands sat astride a vast range of mountains. Along the peaks of these mountains, the Greeks had constructed a 200 kilometer line of fortifications. Despite repeated attacks from the Ju 87s and their counterparts on the ground, the frontier Greek forts held the line. In fact, two forts that were captured in an early German advance were almost immediately re-taken by a Greek counterattack.

Undaunted, German air and ground forces simply outflanked the frontier defenses by moving farther west into Yugoslavia and coming down behind them. Meanwhile, the Greeks hastily formed a second defensive line farther south, from the Gulf of Salonika towards the Yugoslav border. However, this line, too, did not stretch far enough to stop the German advance. Once again, Allied forces were outflanked and the Greco-British forces found themselves pushed back to the Thermopylae line. The British (and their dominion comrades of the Australian and New Zealand Army Corps who were fighting alongside them) were hit particularly hard by the relentless Stuka attacks. Still, the beleaguered Allies gave nearly as much as they got, inflicting heavy damage on StG 2 and StG 77 with anti-aircraft fire.

Towards the end of their retreat, the Allied forces prepared to make another waterborne evacuation as the British had at Dunkirk. However, the Luftwaffe did everything in its power to prevent the British from reaching the coast. In the days before the Brits reached their designated evacuation ports, German squadrons began scouring the waters in and around the Aegean Sea, bombing virtually everything afloat. Despite this bombardment at sea – and concentrated attacks on key targets farther inland from the evacuation ports – the Allies were successful in evacuating some 45,000 troops from the shores of Greece.

After the fall of Athens and the outlying Greek islands, the island of Crete was next. Hitler tasked his air and paratroop units to carry out the attack, but made it clear that his pending invasion of the Soviet Union would not be delayed by events in Crete. Come June 1, regardless of whether or not Crete had been subdued, all air and ground forces tapped for Operation *Barbarossa* would be withdrawn to the Eastern Front.

In the days leading up to the invasion, the *Stukagruppen* increased their raids along Crete's northern coastline; paying particular attention to the island's three landing grounds and to Suda Bay. In fact, on May 18, it was at Suda Bay where Ju 87s from StG 2 damaged the Royal Fleet Auxiliary ship *Olna*, a Royal Navy tanker ship which carried fuel reserves for its parent fleet. Three days later, the Ju 87s were called upon to intercept a British naval task force which had prevented the *Kreigsmarine* from reinforcing Crete. The Stukas' succeeded in destroying the HMS *Juno*, HMS *Greyhound*, and HMS *Gloucester* while severely damaging the HMS *Fiji*. On May 24, Stukas attacked the Crete defenders at Kastelli Bay while the 5th *Panzerdivision* attempted landing their light tanks on the shores. Later that afternoon, the Stukas dive-bombed the capital city of Canea. Although the Stukas had qualitatively won the opening skirmish, four Ju 87s had been lost by day's end.

North Africa

A number of Ju 87s were assigned to assist Rommel's efforts with the *Afrika Korps*. Throughout the North African campaign, the Stuka's magnum opus was during the siege of Tobruk, one of the critical Allied strongholds in Libya. Tobruk came under attack from Rommel's forces in a siege that lasted nearly eight months. The defenders – mostly British and Australian – tenaciously held out against the onslaught of Rommel's three-dimensional beatings.

From the sky, the Stuka relentlessly bombed the town proper, its defenses, and the ships in the nearby harbor. In fact, some of the Stukas' most memorable missions were directed against incoming shipping. In April 1941, during the opening month of the siege, the attendant Stuka forces received two notable maritime missions. The first, occurring on April 12, intercepted a purported supply ship off the coast. However, the mission ended rather indecisively. Although the vessel was reportedly hit, it succeeded in downing one of the attacking Stukas. According to one of the other Stuka crews aloft that day, the ill-fated Ju 87 crashed "into the sea a few hundred meters astern of the target [because] the ship had fired some sort of parachute rocket dragging a length of wire behind it!"

A group of Stukas in flight over the deserts of North Africa on their way to attack British tanks at Ghobi. (Imperial War Museum MH 5591)

Three Allied soldiers stand atop a downed Ju 87 near Tobruk in Libya, 1941. Tobruk saw some of the most intense fighting of the North African campaign. The *Afrika Korps* attempted a siege of Tobruk in 1941, which failed when Operation *Crusader* pushed the Axis forces back out of Cyrenaica. The *Afrika Korps* succeeded in capturing the city in June 1942 until the Allies recaptured it the following November. During these skirmishes, the Stuka performed many of its classic dive-bomb missions, but often fell victim to the Allies' anti-aircraft guns. (State Library of South Australia)

The second mission, on April 17, saw a dozen Ju 87s under the command of veteran pilot officer Helmut Mahlke intercept a supposed "battleship" that had purportedly been shelling the forward army positions near Halfaya Pass. Mahlke led the dozen Stukas in textbook formation towards the target, but as he maneuvered his plane into the dive, he began to wonder if the vessel had been correctly identified. It didn't much resemble a typical Allied battleship, but as he got closer, he saw structures that resembled turret armaments. Erring on the side of military necessity, Mahlke released his 500kg bomb from an altitude of 300m. In his after-action report, Mahlke reported that his target had been a "warship or armed merchantman [vessel]…probably old coastal monitor, sunk in the area NE of Sollum." The identity of the ship, however, remains a mystery. Based on Mahlke's report, the vessel seemed to fit the description of a typical Insect-class river gunboat of the Royal Navy, but none were reported lost on that date.

These peculiar maritime engagements continued into May. On the 12th of that month, a Ju 87 attack on Tobruk harbor sank the HMS *Ladybird*, another Insect-class gunboat. However, the shallow depths of the harbor prevented the upper decks of the *Ladybird* from sinking below the surface, and crew continued to man the turrets throughout the engagement. Fortunately for the Allies at Tobruk, the hull of the *Ladybird* (and its above-water armaments) provided a useful gun battery defense for the harbor.

On May 25, the Ju 87s were airborne again, this time to sink the SS *Helka*, a large civilian tanker that was delivering petrol to the beleaguered defenders at Tobruk. In the same bombardment, these Stukas also crippled her escort, the HMS *Grimsby*. The following month, Ju 87s from both the Luftwaffe and the *Regia Aeronautica* were called upon to repulse the British attempts to re-supply Tobruk from the sea. On June 29, 1941, two British destroyers, the HMS *Waterhen* and HMS *Defender*, were picked up by seven Picchiatello (i.e. Italian-based) Stukas. Leading these Italian Ju 87s was none other than Giuseppe Cenni – who had developed the infamous method of skipping bombs along the surface of the ocean to hit their targets.

Employing his trademark "stone-skipping" tactic, Cenni scored a direct hit on the lead destroyer. The *Waterhen*, though mortally wounded, managed to stay afloat until capsizing the following day. The Italian Ju 87s struck again on July 30 when they intercepted the Royal Navy submarine *Cachalot* while it was surfaced. The ensuing attack damaged the submarine so badly that it could no longer submerge. Now crippled, the *Cachalot* became easy prey for the Italian destroyer that subsequently rammed and sank her.

Meanwhile, on the shores of Tobruk, elements of StG 1 and StG 2 continued harassing the Allied defenders. As there were no fighter aircraft in the immediate area, the aerial engagements became a simple matter of dive-bombers versus high-volume air defense. By this stage, however, the air raids had begun to take their toll on the Stuka crews. More anti-aircraft guns were slipping through the Axis perimeter every week, and the gun crews were steadily improving their techniques. "Instead of concentrating a box barrage at a specific height above the harbour area," said historian John Weal, "the defenders 'thickened the belt' by altering the ceiling and spreading the pattern over an altitude of 1,000 metres or more, thus forcing the Ju 87s to brave the barrage for a much longer period during their dives. And to counter the Stukas' trick of coming down along the edge of the barrage and then sliding under it, the gunners also directed their fire from side to side. A pilot might start his dive clear of the barrage and then find it had swung into his line of flight. Perversely, many Stuka crews took these 'improvements' to be a sign of the enemy's weakening; 'Defensive fire is no longer so well-disciplined and much more ragged at the edges.'" It was as if the Axis pilots couldn't even fathom the possibility of being on the losing end of an engagement.

In September 1941, a peculiar incident transpired with a group of 12 Italian Ju 87s. Under the watchful eyes of a Bf 109 escort, the Picchiatello sortie flew eastward to cover an Axis reconnaissance near Sidi Barrani. However, the Ju 87s lost their fighter escorts and, soon thereafter, lost their bearings too. To make matters worse, ten of the Ju 87s ran out of fuel and forced-landed into the desert.

A German ground crew dismantling a damaged Stuka. As with many of the *Luftwaffe*'s tactical aircraft, the Stuka did not mesh well with the desert environment and the crews made great efforts to ensure that their planes remained functional in the harsh climate. (Bundesarchiv, Bild 146-1981-064-16A)

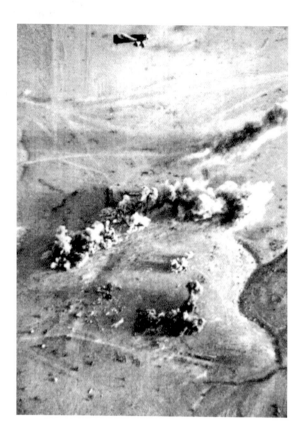

A lone Stuka bombs the perimeter of Fort Pilastrino, one of the primary fortifications defending Tobruk, 1941. (Luftwaffe RFI)

Eight of the crew were captured by the British; and the RAF soon learned that one of these Ju 87s had landed intact near Fort Maddalena. Subsequently, two RAF officers were granted permission to locate the aircraft and fly it back, if possible. After two days of searching, the pair discovered the wayward Stuka, still fully-loaded and relatively unscathed from its forced landing. Although the control panel was still labeled in German, the two RAF officers had little trouble starting the "crate" and getting her airborne. However, after a mere 15 minutes into their flight, the Ju 87's engine sputtered to a halt. Miraculously, though, the pilot landed the plane into the desert sand with nothing more severe than a blown-out tire. After some piecemeal troubleshooting, the two RAF fliers were airborne again. But after a few more minutes, the hydraulic gauge exploded, forcing their crate to land once again.

The next morning, they took off on foot towards Sidi Barrani. Before leaving, however, they scratched the following message into the side of the plane: "This Ju 87 is RAF property. DO NOT TOUCH. W/Cdr Bowman and S/Ldr Rozier left here at dawn 19/9/41 [British short-hand notation for September 19, 1941] walking north." After encountering some nearby friendly forces during their trek, the pair returned to the wrecked plane with two RAF technicians in tow. Following some minor repairs to the engine and a new wheel, the crew was airborne again.

Two months after the curious case of the RAF flyers, Allied troops launched their counter-offensive against Rommel. Dubbed Operation *Crusader*, British and Commonwealth forces succeeded in re-capturing the territory they had lost earlier in the year. And now that the Allied fighter planes had achieved parity with the Axis, the Stukas began suffering heavier losses. November 20, 1941 was a particularly dreadful day for the *Stukagruppen* in North Africa: six planes were reported damaged or destroyed that morning while another 18 Ju 87s were lost that afternoon. On the 30th, 15 Stukas were either shot down or claim as probable losses.

Because of the Allied fighters, several Ju 87s never even reached their targets. One British veteran who had seen the Stuka's comparative performance during the Mediterranean and North African campaigns had this to say:

Now we had a completely different angle on dive-bombers. In Greece and Crete all the talk was of Stukas. Men with no air cover at all were dive-bombed for hours on end in

F   Stukas are attacked by a Spitfire IX while on patrol over the Mediterranean, 1943. After the Nazis failed to conquer Great Britain, they shifted many of their operations southward to the Mediterranean. The Italian *Regia Aeronautica* already had a few Ju 87s, which they used against the Allies in the Mediterranean and North Africa (albeit in small numbers). Meanwhile, the *Luftwaffe* used the Stuka to great effect during the invasions of Yugoslavia and Crete. Hitler also deployed the Stukas to assist Mussolini during the latter's misadventures in Greece and the Balkans. However, by late in the war the Stukas were very vulnerable to Allied fighters.

the trenches and gun emplacements. In Greece, I remember, there was a theory that it was not worthwhile firing back at Stukas because they were armoured against rifle and machine-gun bullets. The result was that they did what they were meant to do – keep men in the slit-trenches, and therefore, out of the battle.

The Allied defenders were confined to trenches and gun emplacements. In those circumstances, the Stuka was successful inasmuch as it kept the troops held up in those fortifications. The Allies' disposition in North Africa, however, was decidedly different. Because of the flat and featureless terrain, tactical vehicles and troop emplacements could be widely spread out. The biggest target a Stuka could hope for in that environment was a single tank or tactical truck. The same British veteran quoted above also remarked that, "This time, we had air superiority, and the dive-bomber had no chance against a fast fighter. So the Germans began to use their Stukas warily and infrequently. Few people got more than two or three bouts of dive-bombing in the course of the whole campaign." On December 7, 1941 (the same day as the attack on Pearl Harbor), the siege of Tobruk finally ended in an Allied victory.

Although the Stuka's heyday in North Africa had now come to an end, the Luftwaffe nevertheless kept the Ju 87 on the front lines until the end of the campaign. During Rommel's surprise counteroffensive in early 1942, the Stukas ran ahead of his advancing columns to attack the Allies' retreat and disrupt their lines of communication. By the end of May, the Stukas had scored some token victories against the Allied defenses along the Gazala Line, but suffered inevitable losses of their own which further depleted their numbers.

After he successfully re-captured Tobruk, Rommel then set his sights on El Alamein. Although he expected El Alamein to be a decisive Axis victory, he underestimated both the terrain and the defenses surrounding El Alamein.

The derelict carcass of a Ju 87 stands on its nose in the North African desert. This Stuka most likely crash-landed at a low altitude. (San Diego Air and Space Museum)

Still, the airborne Stukas pummeled the British lines with their usual tenacity. But by now, the RAF routinely intercepted the Luftwaffe's radio traffic and, with increased fighter presence, they continued to whittle away at the remaining Stukas in theater. In fact, the Stukas frequently had to jettison their bombs early and return to base without reaching their targets. But even within the confines of the air base, the Stuka pilots found little solace as they were often targeted by marauding Allied fighter-bombers. By October 1942, the tides had once again shifted in the Allies' favor. Following the Eighth Army's counterattack, Allied fighters took to the sky and claimed 40 Ju 87s as confirmed kills.

Two poignant events from the fall of 1942 clearly illustrate the end of the Stuka's career in the African desert. On the morning of November 11, as Eighth Army stormed across Libya, a sortie of 15 Stukas made one last attempt to harass the Allied advance. They were quickly intercepted by a squadron of South African P-40s, which destroyed 12 of the Ju 87s, while the remaining three were shot down by a group of American P-40s later that day. Barely a week later, on November 26, tanks from the US 1st Armored Division broke through the Axis line to the Djedeida Airfield where a group of grounded Ju 87Ds lay virtually unprotected. Charging full speed ahead, the American tanks proceeded to shoot up the helpless "Doras" and even managed to crush a few of them under their tank tracks.

Rommel's last offensive against the Allies in North Africa occurred on March 6, 1943, at the battle of Medenine. However, by March 9, the assault had fallen apart and Rommel was replaced soon thereafter by General Hans-Jürgen von Arnim. During these final days of the *Afrika Korps*, the Stukas went airborne only if there enough cloud cover to escape detection from Allied fighters. By April 12, under pressure from the Allied attacks, the remaining Ju 87s began to evacuate North Africa. Finally, on May 13, 1943, the exhausted Hans-Jürgen von Arnim surrendered his beaten and tattered forces to the Allies.

The Eastern Front

Nazi Germany and the Soviet Union had held an uneasy partnership during the opening days of World War II. Neither side trusted the other, but Hitler and Stalin had nonetheless signed a non-aggression pact which (on paper) prevented them both from taking armed action against the other. Hitler, however, had no intention of abiding by it. Thus, on June 22, 1941, Hitler launched an invasion of the Soviet Union, codenamed Operation *Barbarossa*.

By 1941, the Stuka's once-fearsome reputation had been destroyed. Withdrawn from the skies over Britain, the Stuka regained some of its former glory during the Mediterranean and North African campaigns. But when the Allies gained air superiority in those theaters as well, it seemed that the Stuka had nothing more to offer Hitler's war effort. On the Eastern Front, however, the Stuka found a new lease of life as a "tank buster." Generalmajor Hubertus Hitschhold states that:

> missions for anti-tank units were flown only on special centers of resistance along the front, and long rest periods repeatedly arose for them. Anti-tank flying units with their special weapons were used against tanks and armored vehicles which had broken through. For use against tank assembly areas they were not suitable, because these areas were usually heavily protected with A.A [anti-aircraft batteries]. In pursuit, their use against parts of split up tank units was good. For operations of anti-tank units, ground and air defense were specially considered, but weather conditions were of less

Although bridges were difficult targets for the Stuka to destroy, the bridges along the Eastern Front featured heavily on the Stukas' target list. The *Luftwaffe* targeted several bridges along the rivers between Poland and Moscow to trap and destroy the retreating Soviet forces. (Luftwaffe RFI)

importance. Even in very bad weather with low ceiling, anti-tank units could carry out effective and successful raids. Because of the mobility of tanks, finding them in a short space of time was often hard. Especially in fluid situations, exact reports and locations about the appearance of tanks were seldom available. The operations of anti-tank units therefore usually took place like a free sweep attack, in which the aircraft first had to find the tanks in a large target area. Therefore, training in recognition of tanks was especially important for the anti-tank flyers.

During the early stages of *Barbarossa*, the Soviet Air Force had yet to mount a coherent counteroffensive against the Luftwaffe. Thus, with the enemy's air superiority still in the making, the Stuka could enjoy a string of easy victories.

Seven *Stukagruppen* were assigned to cover the initial invasion. They were instructed to provide close air support to *Panzergruppen* 2 and 3, the armored thrust of the Nazi invasion. On the first day of the invasion, the Luftwaffe dominated the skies over Russia. More than 300 Soviet aircraft were shot down, most of which fell prey to the Bf 109. Marauding fighter units also destroyed several hundred Soviet Air Force planes that were still on the ground.

On the opening day of *Barbarossa*, Helmut Mahlke, commander of III./StG 1, was assigned to the first wave. Arriving on the tails of their sister squadron, II./StG 1, Mahlke recalled his first foray into Soviet airspace:

We crossed the border – a peculiar feeling. A new theatre of war, a new foe, but at first, all remained quiet. The Soviets appeared to be fast asleep! The first bombs from II./StG 1 detonate some way off in front of us. Then it's our turn. A few stray puffs of smoke blossom in the sky. The enemy flak has finally woken up. But the gunner's aim is so wild and uncertain that old Stuka hands such as ourselves pay little heed.

The pilots have spotted their targets. Attack! We dive almost vertically, one after the other in quick succession. In a few seconds it's all over. The ruins of the [Red Army] HQ buildings are shrouded in dust, smoke, and flames. We get back into formation and head for home.

The Stukas that day flew into combat equipped with the SD 10 anti-personnel bomb, targeting enemy airfields and troop formations. During this time, the Luftwaffe reported only two Ju 87s lost to enemy fire, while a third was lost to "other causes."

Within 24 hours, the tanks of *Panzergruppen* 2 and 3 were smashing through the Soviet defense en route to Minsk. Supporting this armored strike, the Stukas reverted to their traditional role of "flying artillery" – supporting the friendly ground component by the clearing the way ahead and preventing the enemy from counterattacking by disrupting his communication and supply lines.

On the northern flank of the Germans' front, StG 1 went into action destroying a number of railway targets, including trains carrying light tanks and field guns from Vilnius. On the southern flank, StG 77 bombarded the Soviet citadel of Brest-Litovsk. The fortress and its heavy guns stood within firing distance of the Germans' main supply route – and the Luftwaffe, therefore, was determined to bomb it into submission. However, with its meter-thick walls (already proven impervious to artillery fire), not even the Stukas could break down the defenses of Brest-Litovsk. In the weeklong bombardment that followed, the entire *Geschwader* (nearly 100 Stukas in total) pounded away at the stubborn fortress. Their attack culminated with the delivery of several 600kg bombs – all to no avail. It was not until the twin-engine Ju 88s dropped their 1,800kg "Satan" bombs that the Soviet defenders finally quit.

During these opening weeks of *Barbarossa*, the Luftwaffe made short order of the Soviet Air Force, claiming over 2,000 enemy aircraft destroyed. For example, as 2 and 3 *Panzergruppen* tightened their noose around Minsk, the Luftwaffe fighters intercepted nearly every Soviet bomber that tried to blast open an egress route for the beleaguered Red Army. The fighter units' handiwork enabled the Stukas to bomb within the *Panzergruppen* perimeter – targeting enemy troop formations, armored columns, tactical bridges and railways. These operations took a heavy toll on the Soviet ground forces and displayed the Stuka's effectiveness as a ground-attack aircraft. For instance, on July 5, 1941, Stukas from StG 77 destroyed 18 railcars and over 500 tactical vehicles. As the Germans crossed the Dnieper River en route to Kiev, the Ju 87 once again proved to be a formidable ground-strafing aircraft. On September 13, StG 1 destroyed large swathes of the surrounding railway network and inflicted heavy casualties on the retreating Soviet columns.

A pair of Stukas from II./StG 77 position themselves into a second dive over another target. To the left, the bombs from their first dive have already detonated in a spectacular explosion. The two black dots seen above the Stukas are Soviet armored vehicles that have broken ranks from their convoy. According the pilots' report, both of these vehicles were destroyed. (Luftwaffe RFI)

A few days later, the Stukas of StG 2 saw their first action against the Soviet Navy. The flagships of the Soviet Baltic Fleet (which resided at Kronstadt harbor near Leningrad) were the *Marat* and the *Oktyabrskaya Revolutsia*: two well-known battleships of World War I vintage. Despite their age, both ships packed a devastating punch – their main armament consisted of a dozen 12in. (305mm) guns in four triple turrets. Besides these two formidable battleships, the Baltic Fleet also had an assortment of modern destroyers and cruisers, each with enough firepower to inflict heavy casualties on the German positions along the Leningrad front. In StG 2's sortie against the Baltic Fleet on September 23, Hans-Ulrich Rudel (the now-legendary Stuka ace) sank the battleship *Marat* with a single 1,000kg bomb. In the same attack, the destroyers *Minsk* and *Steregushchiy* also sank along with submarine *M-74*. The *Oktyabrskaya Revolutsia*, however, survived the engagement but was severely damaged.

By October, the Germans were closing in on Moscow. On the battlefront, StG 77 assisted Army Group Centre in its drive towards the Soviet capital. However, the onset of the harsh Russian winter had begun to take its toll on the ill-prepared German forces and, by mid-December, the invaders now found themselves on the defensive. Still, the Stukas of StG 77 were able to boost their beleaguered comrades' morale by inflicting heavy damage on the Soviet defenders. From December 13–22, StG 77 destroyed 23 tanks and over 400 tactical vehicles.

Although their counterparts on the ground had not fared too well in the later stages of *Barbarossa*, the various *Stukageschwader* had earned an impressive combat record. In some ways, it made up for the Stuka's dismal showing in the later campaigns of the Western Front. StG 77 finished the campaign as the top-performing *Geschwader*; they had destroyed 2,401 vehicles, 234 tanks, 92 artillery emplacements, and 21 trains; only 25 Stukas were lost to enemy fire. StG 1 and StG 2 respectively lost 60 and 39 Ju 87s to enemy fire.

In early 1942, the Stukas rendered valuable close air support to the German Army during the battle of the Kerch Peninsula. Since the Germans still had air superiority at this point in the campaign, the Stukas of StG 77 operated with

A lone Stuka in flight over Stalingrad, October 1942. Stalingrad marked the turning point for the Axis in the east. After the Germans' failed summer offensive (*Fall Blau*), they were decisively defeated by the Red Army at Stalingrad. Following that battle, the Germans were on their heels as the Soviets pushed them back into the Reich. (Bundesarchiv, Bild 183-J20510)

Sporting its winter camouflage, an obviously battered Stuka receives some much-needed field repairs before being sent back into action against the Red Army. (Bundesarchiv, Bild 1011-393-1409-18)

impunity as they hammered elements of the Soviet 44th Army landing on the Kerch Peninsula. Indeed, within the first ten days of the battle, the Ju 87s had destroyed half of the Soviet landing force. Later, during the siege of Sevastopol, StG 77 flew more than 7,000 sorties against the Soviet defenders and dropped more than 3,500 metric tons of ordnance on the city. Their efforts facilitated the Soviet surrender of the city on July 4, 1942.

The following month, the battle of Stalingrad proved to be the high point for the Stuka along the Eastern Front. Considered among the bloodiest battles in the history of warfare, the Ju 87s played an integral part in the early stages of the German offensive. Stukas from StG 1, StG 2, and StG 77 flew more than 1,000 sorties in support of the German Sixth Army. Stuka operations helped the advancing Germans by silencing the Soviet artillery on the banks of the Volga River, but after the Soviets were pushed into a narrow 1,000ft enclave along the west bank, they retaliated with a winter counteroffensive which was largely credited with turning the tides of the war along the Eastern Front. Although the Stukas averaged about 500 sorties per day, and inflicted heavy damage on the Soviet formations, they still could not prevent the breakout from Stalingrad.

After Stalingrad, the Soviet Air Force began to wrest air superiority from the Luftwaffe over the Eastern Front. StG 1, StG 2, and StG 3 committed its Stukas to support the battle of Kursk, the largest tank battle in history. Although the Ju 87G had a devastating effect on Soviet armor at Orel and Belgorod, Stuka losses were considerably high – one unit reporting as many as 30 aircraft lost within one month. As the Stuka losses mounted, the Luftwaffe began converting the dive-bomb units into direct-fire ground attack units equipped with the new Focke-Wulf Fw 190. As a stop-gap measure, the remaining Stuka units performed their missions under heavy fighter escorts.

Following the German defeat at Kursk, the Ju 87s continued to play a vital role along the southern end of the Eastern Front. Despite growing losses from a resurgent Soviet Air Force, the Stukas did assist the German XXIX *Armeekorps* in their breakout from the Sea of Azov. However, in the aftermath of Kursk, the number of Ju 87s on-hand fell to a mere 184. This number put the combined Stuka force at less than 50 percent of its required strength. As more Stuka units converted to the Fw 190, they lost the *Stukageschwader* designation – StG 1, StG 2, StG 3, StG 5, and StG 77 were all re-designated *Schlachtgeschwader* (SG) units, reflecting their new ground attack role. With this new classification, the Luftwaffe's dive-bomber units ceased to exist. The Stuka's last hurrah in the east was in the summer of 1944, when several Ju 87s arrived on the Finnish front as part of the *Gefechtsverband Kuhlmey*, an aerial task force also consisting of several Fw 190s and Bf 109s. The unit was instrumental in halting the Soviet's Karelian Offensive (and claimed 200 Soviet tanks destroyed) but, by this juncture, the Luftwaffe's operations were having little effect on the greater ground war.

By the spring of 1945, barely 100 Stukas remained operational. Fuel shortages, however, kept most of them grounded until Nazi Germany surrendered on May 8, 1945.

Service with the air forces of Eastern Europe

Romania

The Romanian Air Force was the largest foreign operator of Stukas along the Eastern Front. Ironically, however, the Romanians never *owned* a single Ju 87 – they were all placed on loan from the Luftwaffe. It also took several requests from the Romanian government to secure these "loaners." As early as 1939, the Romanians had asked for 60 Ju 87s, but Hitler perennially refused their requests. Once Operation *Barbarossa* began to lose its momentum, however, Hitler relented and approved the delivery of 45 Ju 87s to Nikolayev, where the Romanian air crews waited to receive their new mounts.

Grupul 3, the first Romanian Air Force unit to fly the Stuka in combat, flew its first sortie on June 17, 1943. With its ten Stukas, Grupul 3 attacked two villages that were occupied by Soviet troops. All ten Ju 87s returned from the mission, but the Romanians lost their first Stuka the following morning to anti-aircraft fire.

The following month, Grupul 3 provided bomber support for the Axis ground forces holding the Kuban bridgehead on the Kerch Straits. Although Grupul 3 lost two aircraft on its first mission over the Kerch Straits, the Romanian air crews decisively proved themselves in what has since been described as the best tactical air support the *Wehrmacht* ever received from an Axis partner. Still, the campaign took a heavy toll on the Romanian Stukas. By October, 33 aircraft had been damaged and nine Ju 87s had been lost. Later that month, Grupul 3 tried to disrupt the Soviet advance in the Crimea. Over the next six months, the Stukas of Grupul 3 flew nearly 1,500 missions while losing only 15 planes.

By May 20, 1943, another Romanian air unit, Grupul 6, had been stationed at Husi, adding its 28 Ju 87Ds to the 25 of Grupul 3, which were stationed at Recuci, some 60 miles (100 km) away. This relocation soon prompted Grupul 3 and Grupul 6 to operate together. The synergy of these Romanian

dive-bomber units brought some devastating firepower to the nearby Soviet formations. On May 30, Grupul 3 and 6 mounted 93 sorties – losing only four Ju 87s in the process. The following day, 69 Stukas took flight to attack some heavily-concentrated armor and artillery formations. In the midst of keeping the Red Army at bay, the Romanian pilots were promised to receive retraining on the newer, more agile Focke-Wulf Fw 190. However, Romania's allegiances were about to take an unexpected turn.

Stukas in flight over the Eastern Front on December 22, 1943. By this point in the war, the Soviets had re-gained the initiative and were steadily rolling the Nazi tide back into Germany. (Bundesarchiv, Bild 101I-646-5188-17)

On August 20, the Red Army launched its full-scale invasion of Romania. The Stukas of Grupul 3 and 6 once again took flight, dive-bombing and strafing the enemy columns, but the horde of Soviet troops proved too much for the Romanian defense. Three days after the invasion, the Romanians accepted a cease-fire. The following day, in a surprising turn of events, a group of indignant Luftwaffe personnel re-acquired the Stukas from Grupul 6 and flew their own reprisal raids over Bucharest.

When the new (pro-Soviet) Romanian government declared war against Germany on August 25, many of the pilots from Grupul 3 suddenly found themselves flying alongside the Soviet Air Force in raids against the *Wehrmacht*. Under command of the 5th Soviet Air Force, the Romanian Stukas saw limited action against retreating German and Hungarian forces in the Carpathian Mountains. However, the lack of spare parts and trained technicians gradually reduced the Ju 87's effectiveness within the Russo-Romanian units. Indeed, by the end of the war, the Romanians had only nine functional Ju 87s on hand.

Hungary

Like the Romanians, Hungary had also solicited Hitler for a contingent of Stukas. However, the Führer was more accommodating to Hungary than he had been to Romania. He did not reject the Hungarians' appeal, but waited nearly two years to deliver the first batch of Ju 87s. However, it soon became clear that Hitler had misplaced his trust in the Hungarian Air Force. By 1942, he had deemed their performance so lackluster, that he cancelled their outstanding order for 26 additional Ju 87s. When the Hungarians requested further Messerschmitts, Hitler reportedly said: "If I am to part with aircraft, then I'd rather they went to the Croats, as they've at least proved they know how to attack. With the Hungarians all we've had so far are fiascos."

However, just as it had been with the Romanians, Hungary did not receive more Stukas until the tides had turned against Germany on the Eastern Front. In early 1943, 12 Ju 87Ds arrived in Hungary. These aircraft formed the backbone of Hungary's 102/2 Dive-bomber Squadron. In the fall of 1943, the 102/2 was placed under operational control of the Luftwaffe's II./StG 77. In this capacity, they flew over 1,000 sorties and dropped more than 800 tons of ordnance (and even claimed to have shot down three Soviet fighters). Nevertheless, these operations took a heavy toll on 102/2, and the unit lost several of its aircraft during the ensuing months.

By the summer of 1944, the Hungarian squadron, now re-numbered 2/2, had been transferred to the Nazi airbase at Kuniow in German-occupied Poland. This move, however, put them directly in the path of the Red Army's counteroffensive, which itself led to the collapse of Army Group Centre and cleared the Soviets' path to Berlin. One week after the Soviets launched their offensive, the 2/2 Stukas flew their first mission out of the German-held airbase. The following month, they retired to Krosno, where the tenant Luftwaffe unit was converting its Ju 87 fleet to the newer Fw 190. From Krosno and other nearby bases, 2/2 carried out several missions over the next few months. By the fall of 1944, they had emerged from their bombing raids with seven of their initial 12 aircraft.

In September, the Hungarian squadron returned to its homeland, but the following month most of its aircraft were destroyed on the ground during a strafing run by American P-51s. This hunter-killer strike effectively ended the Stuka's career in the Hungarian Air Force, although the Hungarians reportedly conducted a few small-scale attacks on Soviet armored columns throughout the winter of 1944 and into the early months of 1945.

A Stuka from StG 77 over the Eastern Front, 1943. As the Soviets regained air superiority over their homeland, the Stuka once again fell prey to enemy fighters. Even under its own fighter escort, however, it became clear that the Stuka's role as dive-bomber had become obsolete. By the end of 1944, most of the *Stukageschwader* units had converted to ground-attack units equipped with the Fw 190. (Bundesarchiv, Bild 101I-630-3561-27)

Bulgaria

Bulgaria's participation on the Eastern Front was reluctant at best. Although the Bulgarians received nearly 50 Ju 87s from the Luftwaffe, King Boris refused to go to war against the Soviet Union. Nevertheless, a modest group of 15 Bulgarian pilots received training at the Stuka schools in Bad Aibling and Wertheim, Germany.

The first Ju 87s arrived in Bulgaria in August 1943. Theses R-variants were primarily used as trainers until a new shipment of 32 Ju 87Ds arrived. These "Dora" variants formed the backbone of a Bulgarian squadron that conducted operations against home-grown partisan units and those across the border in Yugoslavia. Bulgaria, however, was about to suffer a similar fate to Romania.

Bulgaria suddenly "withdrew" from the war on August 26, 1944. However, its self-declared neutrality was not to last; the Soviets were already at Bulgaria's border. When the Red Army invaded a few days later, the Bulgarians quietly accepted a new pro-Soviet government and declared war on Germany shortly thereafter. Following their change of allegiance, the Bulgarian pilots flew alongside the Soviet Air Force in sorties against their former allies. "Thus, as historian John Weal pointed out, "the only frontline operations ever undertaken by Bulgarian Stukas were the few ground-attack sorties reportedly flown against their former allies as Axis troops withdrew from Yugoslavia at the end of 1944."

Croatia

Of Axis partners who operated the Stuka, Hitler was perhaps most complimentary of the Croats. Still, the Croats were at the shallow end of the Stuka allotment. Indeed, the Slavic nation never had more than 15 Ju 87s. The Croats' only Stuka squadron saw limited action in East Prussia during the summer of 1944, but its operational history on that front remains sketchy. What *is* known, however, is that ten of the Croats' 14 aircraft had been rendered unserviceable by October 1944. By early November, the Croatian pilots were ordered to relinquish their remaining aircraft to the Luftwaffe. Thus ended Croatia's brief and undistinguished history with the Ju 87.

Slovakia

The Slovakian Air Force, while small, had proven itself in the early stages of *Barbarossa*. Despite their praises from Adolf Hitler, however, the Slovakian Air Force did not receive any Stukas until 1944, when the Red Army's spring offensive came to the foot of the Carpathian Mountains. The Slovakians' No 11 and No 12 Squadron were subsequently ordered to convert to Ju 87Ds. The first three "Doras" to be delivered, however, were purportedly used to form a mixed squadron, along with three native Letov light bombers, that flew several ground-attack missions against the invading Soviets. By June 1944, No 11 reportedly had 12 Stukas on hand and Junkers reportedly delivered 11 more Ju 87s in August.

On August 28, however, Slovakia found itself in the throes of a national uprising; and a good portion of Slovakia's armed forces sided with the insurgency. Germany, of course, retaliated by invading Slovakia from the west. The nationalists, however, gathered the Ju 87s (along with several other aircraft) to form a "Combined Squadron" at the Tri Duby airfield. Consequently, just as the Germans had seen in Romania and Bulgaria, their own Ju 87s were being flown against them. The Slovak insurgency continued until the Red Army arrived in 1945.

One of the few surviving Stukas on display at the Chicago Museum of Science and Industry, suspended in its dive. The camouflage pattern indicates that this Ju 87 was captured during the North African campaign. By the end of World War II, only 104 Stukas remained operational. (Author's collection)

THE POSTWAR POST-SCRIPT

Following Germany's surrender, the Luftwaffe was disbanded in 1946 by the Allied Control Commission. Subsequently, most of Germany's World War II aircraft (including the Stuka) were destroyed. Nevertheless, there are a few surviving Ju 87s either on display or in various stages of restoration. The two most notable Ju 87s can be seen on display either at the Chicago Museum of Science and Industry or at the Royal Air Force Museum in London.

On mainland Europe, the German Museum of Technology also has two complete Stukas which were recovered from crash sites in Russia during the early 1990s. Also in Germany, the Sinsheim Auto and Technik Museum has on display the remains of a Ju 87 raised from the sea in 1989. It was confirmed to be the wreckage of a Stuka that crashed near Saint-Tropez in 1944. Despite the crash and its long interment underwater, the wings and large portions of the fuselage remain intact. Lastly, at the Yugoslav Aeronautical Museum, a single Ju 87B remains under reconstruction.

FURTHER READING

Since the end of World War II, a number of books have been written about the Junkers Ju 87. From personal memoirs of Stuka pilots, to photographic essays, to multi-volume operational histories, the Ju 87's bibliography is indeed comprehensive.

The celebrated Stuka pilots Hans Ulrich Rudel and Helmut Mahlke wrote of their experiences in their respective memoirs, *Stuka Pilot* and *Memoirs of a Stuka Pilot*. Both provide valuable insights into the lives and careers of two men who were at the forefront of the Stuka's heyday. Rudel was the most highly

Other Stukas have been preserved in various states of disrepair. A notable example is this Ju 87 on display at the Sinsheim Auto & Technik Museum. It crashed into the sea near Saint-Tropez, France in 1944 (possibly during Operation Dragoon) and was recovered from the seabed in 1989. After spending 45 years underwater, barely half of the fuselage remained intact. (LSDSL)

decorated pilot in the Luftwaffe and flew 2,530 combat missions. He was noted for his command of III./StG 2 and his participation in the battle of Kursk. Along with the rest of the *Wehrmacht*, Rudel surrendered to the Allies on May 8, 1945. He remained a prisoner-of-war for the next 11 months. Upon his release, he moved to Argentina in 1948 and remained there until returning to West Germany in 1953. He passed away in 1982. Mahlke was another prominent Stuka ace and was noted for his command of III./StG 1. During the course of his career in the Luftwaffe, Mahlke served with distinction in the Battle of Britain, the invasion of Yugoslavia, and throughout the Eastern Front. Mahlke survived the war and went on to become a general in the West German Air Force. He passed away in 1998 at the age of 85.

Perhaps the best multi-volume treatise to cover the operational history of the Stuka is the trilogy of illustrated books authored by Stuka expert John Weal. Weal is the world's leading expert on the Stuka and possesses a wealth of primary sources relating to the Ju 87 (including operational reports, personal papers, and technical documents) Written for Osprey's *Combat Aircraft* series, these books are: *Junkers Ju 87 Stukageschwader 1937-41*; *Junkers Ju 87 Stukageschwader of North Africa and the Mediterranean*; and *Junkers Ju 87 Stukageschwader of the Russian Front*. All three are beautifully illustrated and contain a number of personal anecdotes provided by the pilots and crew of the Stuka throughout its various campaigns.

Robert Jackson's *Ju 87 Stuka*, written for the Crowood Press's *Combat Legends* series, provides a great discussion on the technical aspects of the Stuka which are absent from many other books on the Ju 87. Another great source for technical data (and highly-detailed illustrations) is Eddie J. Creek's *Junker Ju 87: From Dive-Bomber to Tank-Buster 1935-1945*. Other fine illustrated works include the two-volume *Luftwaffe Ju 87 Dive-Bomber Units* collection by Peter Smith. Both works cover the operational history of the aircraft against the backdrop of some lavish illustrations.

Other notable illustrated works include: *Stukas over Spain* by Rafael Permuy and Lucas Molina, *Stuka: Hitler's Lethal Dive-Bomber* by Alistair Smith, and *Ju 87 Stuka in Action* by Brian Filley, Don Greer, and James G. Robinson. Lastly, *The Stuka – Trumpets of Jericho*, by Bob Carruthers, is a concise history of the Stuka which includes some valuable information on the development of the Stuka's combat tactics.

INDEX

Figures in **bold** refer to illustrations.